Conversations with the World

*American Women Poets
and Their Work*

Conversations with the World

American Women Poets and Their Work

Phebe Davidson

Trilogy Books
Pasadena, California

Publisher's Cataloging in Publication

Conversations with the world: American women poets and their
        work / [edited by] Phebe Davidson. -- 1st ed.
            p. cm.
            ISBN 0-9623879-9-1

        1. American poetry--Women authors. 2. Women poets,
American--Interviews. 3. American poetry--20th century.
4. Poets, American--Interviews. I. Davidson, Phebe.

    PS589.C66 1998   811'.54'0809287
                                            QBI98-33

Library of Congress Catalog Card Number: 98-60025

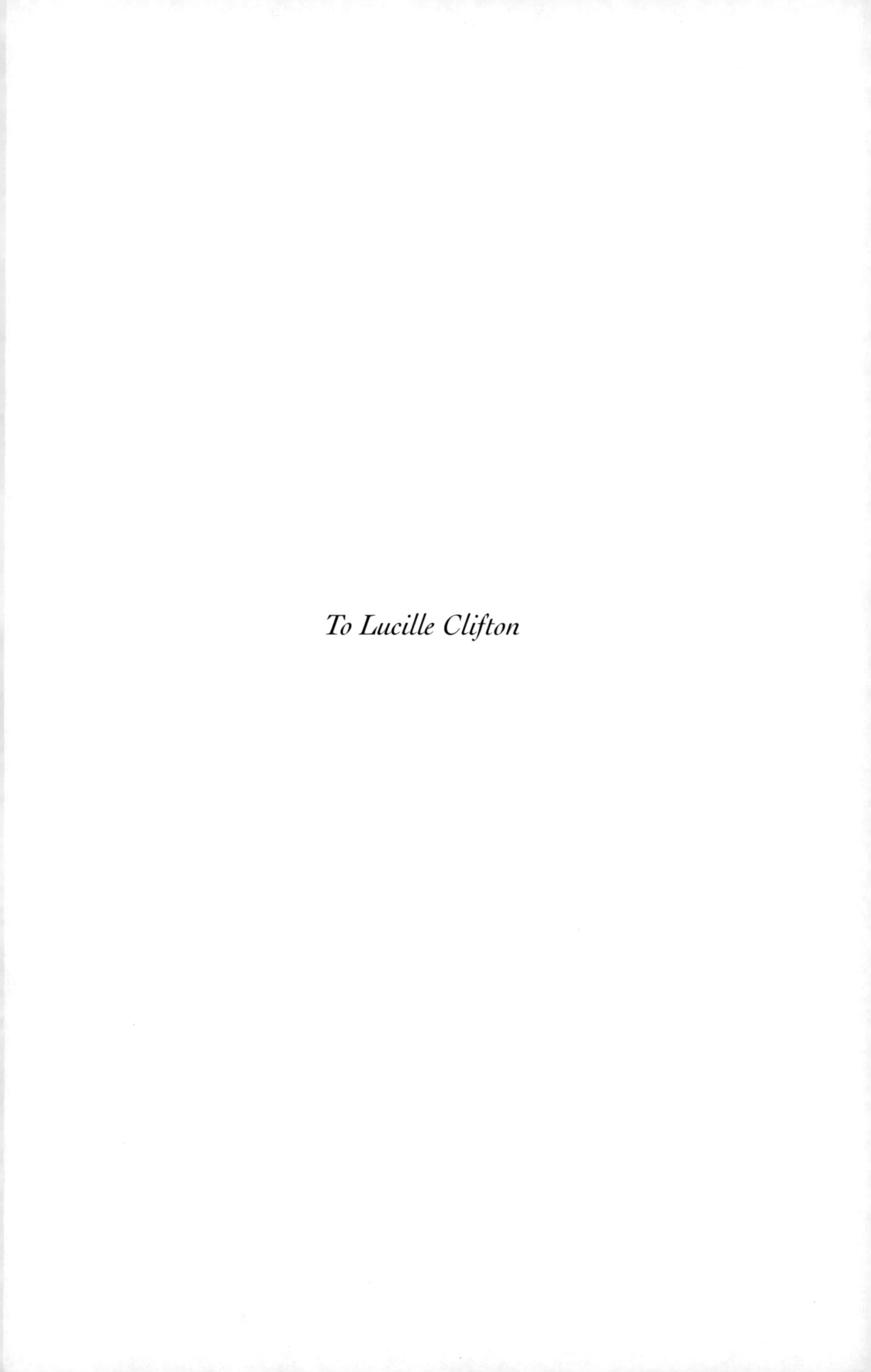

To Lucille Clifton

My personal gratitude to the following individuals who have enriched the time spent working on this book with their generosity, spirited comments, and other intangible wonders. To the women who so willingly shared their time and experience through extended conversations: Karen Swenson, Alicia Suskin Ostriker, Naomi Shihab Nye, Susan Ludvigson, Linda Hogan, Toi Derricotte, and Judith Ortiz Cofer. To my husband Steve. To my good friends and colleagues, without whom I would never get anything done: Liz Bell, Sue Lorch, Steve Gardner, Tom Mack and (in all weathers) Jo Tarvers.

This book has been funded in part by grants from:
The South Carolina Arts Commission
The Vice-Chancellor's Office of the University of South Carolina-Aiken

Contents

The White Rabbit

The Cambodian Box

We

Without Reservations

Offering

Death Dreams

The Dog's Tooth of Faith

Grateful acknowledgement is made to the following authors and publications for permission to reprint selected poems.

Books:

Derricotte, Toi. Captivity. University of Pittsburgh Press, 1989. "Books," "Hamtramck: The Polish Women," "The Friendship," "Allen Ginsberg," "On theTurning Up of Unidentified Black Female Corpses," "A Note on My Son's Face," and "Christmas Eve: My Mother Dressing."

Hogan, Linda. Book of Medicines. Coffeehouse Press, 1993. "The History of Red,"* "Crossings," and "The Origins of Corn."

_______ Calling Myself Home. Greenfield Review Press, 1979. "Hackberry Trees," and "Song for my Name,"

_______. Seeing Through the Sun. University of Massachusetts Press, 1985. "The Truth Is."

Nye, Naomi Shihab. Different Ways to Pray. Breitenbush, 1980. "The Words Under the Words," and "For Mohammed on the Mountain,"

_______ Hugging the Jukebox. National Poetry Series. 1982. "Making a Fist."

_______ Red Suitcase. 1994. "Arabic," "Voices," and "For the 500th Dead Palestinian, Ibtisam Bozieh."

_______ Yellow Glove. 1986. "Yellow Glove," "My Uncle Mohammed at Mecca, 1981," and "Who's Who, 1941."

Ostriker, Alicia Suskin. The Crack in Everything. University of Pittsburgh Press, 1996. The Mastectomy Poems; "The Bridge," "The Gurney," "Mastectomy," "What Was Lost,'"December 3`," "Wintering," "Healing," and "The River."

Swenson, Karen. The Landlady in Bangkok. National Poetry Series. Copper Canyon, 1993. "The Cambodian Box" and "We."

_______. A Sense of Direction. The Smith, 1989. "The White Rabbit."

* Special thanks to **Judy Grahn** for her lines from "A Woman Is Talking to Death."

Magazines and Journals:

Gettysburg Review: "The Gospel According to Mary Magdalen" by **Susan Ludvigson**.

Kenyon Review: "From Penelope's Journal: Learning to Walk Alone" and "The Drowned Sailor" by **Judith Ortiz Cofer**.

Southern Review: "From Penelope's Journal: Dear Odysseus" and "Penelope" by **Judith Ortiz Cofer**.

Salmagundi: "Offering" by **Karen Swenson**.

Snake Nation: "Hagar" by **Judith Ortiz Cofer**.

Thanks as well to the following journals where portions of these conversations first appeared:

The Atlanta Review. "A Necessary Act: A Conversation with Naomi Shihab Nye."

The AWP Chronicle. "An Interview with Linda Hogan."

Belles Lettres. "An Interview with Karen Swenson."

Preface

Ishould like to begin this book the way it actually started, with some personal history. Mine has been, for the most part, a conventional, white, middle-class woman's life. As a youngster I did well in school, but not *too* well; as a teenager I dated, but not *too* much; I was an avid reader, but my childhood and adolescent reading was heavily supervised. Later, as a young woman, I did not challenge the expectations of my age. I became a high school English teacher because I understood perfectly, as so many of my generation did, that publishing and writing weren't really a woman's game.

I fought with my father about my education. A factory worker who had never attended college, he viewed education for a woman as a waste of time. When, in later life, he would brag about my accomplishments, it was always in a tone of surprise. My mother, a college graduate earning less than men in comparable positions in her office, was suspicious of education. She believed it was necessary, but was hard pressed to explain why. As an undergraduate, I believed the professor who told me that no woman had ever written a great work of literature.

By the time I was thirty-nine, I had been married fifteen years. I had a husband. I had two children. I had a house, a car. I had a career as a high school English teacher. And it was okay. It was better than okay. It was, as they say, a life. Complete. Intact. Full. I had no sense that anything was missing and a great sense that when I was unhappy it was because of my own shortcomings.

When my children entered school, I did too. I returned to the world of the academy to "do" a Ph.D. in part because I wanted some change in my routine after the concentrated years of mothering small children, in part because I still wanted to teach but I was heartily sick of high school English, and in part because this degree would put me (I then believed) in a more marketable condition whatever I might choose to do.

Roughly a month and a half after starting graduate studies, I was seated in my living room in my favorite chair. The children were in bed, the dishes were washed, and I looked forward to an evening of reading in an anthology handed to me by one of my professors. I can remember the title without even stopping to think—*The Third Woman*, edited by Dexter Fisher. I had read no more than forty pages when I had to put the book down because I was weeping, sobbing convulsively. My hands weren't steady enough to hold the book, and I could not have seen the print in any case because of my tears. Three words came out of my mouth over and over again.

There they are. There they are. **There they are.**

What had happened was fairly simple. I had simultaneously recognized and begun to fill a tremendous void in my life. I had finally found other women like me, women whose life in language was an absolute passion. Otherwise, these were women whose external lives (and very probably their inner lives as well) were vastly different from my own. These women inhabited reservations and barrios; they knew, intimately, poverty and discrimination in levels I had only conceived as abstractions; they raised their children in circumstances so adverse as to be crippling and they loved whom they would out of strength and necessity alike. These were women I had never, until now, been told about in school.

For the first time in nearly forty years of life, I was **not**, in some telling way, alone. These women's voices, encoded in their texts, brought us together across the barriers of time and geography, class and culture. We were, and are, very different women, but we are none of us as separate as we were.

• • •

I began this project two and half years ago with a sense that it was something important to do, that a record of continuing and serious conversations with an assortment of women poets was something of genuine value to the world. That sense emerged from my personal history and my experience as a reader of contemporary American poetry, by women and by men, which made it excruciatingly clear that women's poetry is not, on the whole, the same as men's.

Today, making that statement, I am astonished not by the fact that I can make the claim so assuredly, but by the fact that many readers still deny its validity. After all, the argument goes, women and men are writing in the same languages about the same cultures, the same issues of personal, regional, national, and global implications. Women and men have access to the same literary traditions, the same formal, technical, even playful aspects of poetic language. And last but not least, there is the canon.

There are, however, major differences in the way that women relate to the shared language, and in the uses to which women are likely to put the formal, technical, and even the playful aspects of a language that is not theirs in quite the same sense that it belongs to their male counterparts. The canon, which is not nearly as male and white as it used to be, continues to change.

Although I will not trace here the history of the suppression of women's right to public discourse, that suppression is a continuing historical reality. And while I have no real desire to hammer away at a point made in venues ranging from the academic conference through scholarly books and journals to popular books and magazines, that suppression is part of the reason this book is necessary.

The writers represented here are, whether considered individually or in combination, formidable. Their names are the literary equivalent of household words. Each of them is a force to be reckoned with in contemporary letters. Each writes with passion, with craft, and with joy. Each has achieved multi-national recognition for her work. Each of them works well in genres outside of poetry, yet each is, and remains, a poet.

Consider, then, the experiences of these poets:

Judith Ortiz Cofer, bi-culturally defined, self-perceived throughout childhood and adolescence as not part of anything around her.

Toi Derricotte, a light-skinned black woman coping with the pressures of a Catholic education and the racial complexity of American society.

Linda Hogan, a woman of mixed blood often more comfortable within her tribal identification than without it, who never believed until she was an adult that formal higher education was a possiblity in her life, a splendid poet who doubts the efficacy of poetry in contemporary life.

Susan Ludvigson, who as a teacher of high school English was convinced that her own creativity had been destroyed by her public education, whose mature work was to lead her to ways of being intellectually alive that are light-years from her midwestern upbringing.

Naomi Shihab Nye, a Palestinian-American whose blessed sense of being at home *everywhere* enables her to speak and write with relative ease, who is acutely aware how easily her sense of at-homeness could have been a sense of dispossession.

Alicia Ostriker, a feminist Jew who credits her own success in formal education to her ability to play the "smart daughter," who only relatively late in her own life discovered the force and regenerative power of women's poetry, the way it gives us to ourselves.

Karen Swenson, a writer who had to overcome the demands placed on her by a society that assessed her by gender rather than by talent in order to achieve the pristine quality of a body of work that has gained her international recognition.

All these women, of course, are exceptional, because each is a gifted and powerful writer. They are not exceptional, however, in their experience of cultural-, class-, ethnic-, and gender-based discrimination in American life and letters.

Yet these women have prevailed as artists, producing work that has won them sufficient recognition to guarantee their success as *artists*, a success that demands acceptance of them as human beings, as women. Their works, which include fiction, essays, and scholarly prose as well as the poems, do not merely chronicle the days in which we live; they also connect our days and our very selves to the mythic substratum from which the days and the selves grow; they make possible deep knowledge and identification and even create the possibility of chance, the belief that despair and the abandonment it implies are not our only options.

Humanity today is haunted by what some have called the postmodern condition. Everything, it seems, is coming apart at an accelerated rate. *Ethnic cleansing. Viral outbreaks. Video wars. Aids. Famine. Global warming.* We face an unprecedented barrage of human and ecological disaster daily. Even the nature of postmodern language has become tormented and convoluted to a degree that makes it all but incomprehensible as it encompasses more and more *post-* notions. *Post-structuralism. Post-formalism. And on and on.* And that, I believe, is why this book and others like it are not only necessary, but profoundly useful. In an age that is defined by the concept of *post-*, of being *after* everything rather than *of* it, we risk adding despair to the growing list of threats to the world and those that dwell in it. We need, more than ever, to know what I discovered in my living room less than fifteen years ago. More than ever, we need to know that we are not alone on this planet, awash in a flood of syntactically tortured abstractions.

There are poets among us, writers who knit us together in mysterious and fundamental ways, who are whole people living on an earth that continues, in spite of everything, to hold us all.

Judith Ortiz Cofer

Drawn to the Outsider

Judith Ortiz Cofer was born in Hormigueros, Puerto Rico on February 24, 1952. Her brother, Rolando Ortiz, was born three years later. The Ortiz children spent their childhood moving back and forth between two places, two cultures. Their father, who had completed a tour of duty with the U.S. Army, joined the Navy. The family made its home in Paterson, New Jersey, but whenever their father was at sea, the children returned to Puerto Rico with their mother. This bifurcated childhood has yielded a rich legacy for Cofer the writer, who explores the meanings of a bi-cultural identity in much of her work.

Cofer's publishing career, which began with a poem in the *New Mexico Humanities Review*, soon turned to larger collections. Among the earliest chapbooks were *Latin Women Pray* (Florida Arts Gazette Press, 1980), *The Native Dancer* (Pteranodon Press, 1981), *Among the Ancestors* (Louisville News Press, 1984), and *Peregrina* (Riverstone Press, 1986), a prizewinning manuscript in the Riverstone International Chapbook Competition in 1986. These were followed by *Reaching for the Mainland, Poems* (Bilingual Press, 1987), which was reprinted by Bilingual Press in 1996 as *Reaching for the Mainland and Selected New Poems*; *Terms of Survival, Poems* (Arte Publico Press, 1987 & 1995); and the novel *Line of the Sun* (University of Georgia Press, 1989; Spanish translation by Elena Olazagasti Segovia, University of Puerto Rico Press, 1996). Subsequently, Cofer produced two collections of mingled poetry and prose, *Silent Dancing* (Arte Publico Press, 1990; *Bailando En Silencio*, Spanish translation by Elena Olazagasti Segovia, Arte Publico Press, 1997), *The Latin Deli* (University of Georgia Press, 1993) and *An Island Like You: Stories of the Barrio* (Orchard Books, 1995; Penguin, 1997), foreign publication forthcoming in Holland, Mexico, and Italy.

Recognition for Cofer's work embraces both her poetry and her prose, and includes such notable successes as a Pushcart Prize nomination by Rita Dove in 1995, a National Book Award Nomination for *The Latin Deli*, which also received the Anisfield-Wolf Book Award in 1994 (shared with Ronald Takaki and David Leering Lewis) and a nomination for the National Magazine Award in fiction by *The Georgia Review* in 1992. Cofer has received an O.Henry prize for "Nada" (1994) and has been listed in *100 Most Notable Short Stories of 1993* ("Not For Sale"), in the 1995 Best American Essays, Notable Essays of the Year List for "Taking the Macho." She has received special mention in *The Pushcart Prize: Best of the Small Press 1993* for her poem "Letter From My Mother in Spanish" and in *Best American Essays* (1992) for "Advanced Biology." *Silent Dancing* received a PEN/Martha Albrand Special Citation in non-fiction. *An Island Like You: Stories of the Barrio* was named a Best Book of the

Year 1995-96 by the American Library Association and awarded the Pura Belpre medal by REFORMA of ALA in 1996. She has received numerous fellowships. Frequently interviewed and anthologized, she yet remains accessible and down to earth.

Subsequent to graduation from high school, Judith Ortiz attended Augusta College where she met and, at the age of nineteen, married John Cofer. Their only child is a daughter, Tanya, who is a second year Ph.D. student at the University of Georgia. Subsequent to her daughter's birth, Cofer completed her B.A. at Augusta College [Augusta State University] and her M.A. in English at Florida Atlantic University. Today, Cofer is still moving between locations, from the University of Georgia in Athens, Georgia, where she is a full professor of English, to the farm in Louisville Georgia where she lives with her family.

How did a Puerto Rican girl from Paterson, New Jersey end up as a professor of English and Creative Writing at the University of Georgia?

(Laughter) Basically, we wanted to get back to Georgia because my husband is from Georgia. Since I had come to Georgia when I was fifteen years old, I had ties here too. I first came to the University of Georgia as an instructor on a three year contract. For various reasons my contract wasn't renewed. Then I took the next four years to write, and then the university asked me back under much more favorable circumstances. In fact, I was just rec-ommended for promotion to full professor; circumstances are making up for the past. This is the best possible arrangement for us because it keeps my family where they want to be. And that's my personal definition of home. It's where the people you love are. That's home, since I don't particularly have one place.

Did you always feel that way?

Paterson was the place where I wanted to be when my family came to Georgia. Of course, at age fifteen I didn't have much say in what my parents were doing. I tell the story in "Advanced

Biology." In 1968, Paterson was a mess. There was tremendous unrest and even race riots. Daddy had retired from the Navy and his two brothers here in Augusta were getting ready to retire from the Army, out of Fort Gordon. They thought Augusta was beautiful, a good place to bring up a family. So we moved down here and the rest is history, as they say. I met my husband during my freshman year at Augusta College, and we married young. Although we lived in Florida for ten years, all he talked about was coming back. So I took the first possible opportunity to get a job to get back. And my daughter was born here in Augusta.

Your daughter with the Russian name. . .?

(Laughter) Yes. That's right. I was reading *Dr. Zhivago* at the time, and you know. . .

That's rather wonderful. It seems to show that for people who read, the things we read are often as real, in some ways, almost as fully fleshed, as the people we live with day to day.

Absolutely!

But you were born in Puerto Rico . . .

I was born on the island while Daddy was away with the Army. Mom was pregnant when he left and he came back when I was two years old. Then he joined the Navy, so we first came to Paterson when I was about two years old. After that we moved back to the island every time Daddy went off to his tours of duty because Mom didn't want to stay in Paterson.

In Line of the Sun *you write about the island with breathtaking immediacy, as if Puerto Rico, the place itself, travels with you always.*

I think it does. The character there says *The island is always with you, like a snail carrying its home on its back.* And of course my most immediate, my most enduring sensory impressions were on the island because in Paterson we lived such a closed, isolated life. Puerto Rico, where Mama's [my grandmother's] house was, was the place where the smells of food and the smells of plants and the noise, all that sensory richness existed. Paterson had its own life, but it was different in a sensory way than Puerto Rico's. So I'm writing of a time before I was born, when things were different from what I knew. The Puerto Rico I grew up in was "operation bootstrap" Puerto Rico. So while the Puerto Rico in the early part of the book has my sensory impressions, I had to do a lot of research for the first part of the book, which dealt with Puerto Rico in the early fifties. But I already had the emotional connection.

As a child, did you find shuttling back and forth between the island and Paterson a hardship? Or was it empowering in some way?

At the time I felt it was very much a hardship. I was always the new kid, and so was my brother, who was three years younger. We became bookworms because my father, who was a very smart man, and who understood the importance of learning and books, insisted that we keep up with our studies. My father would buy the books from the schools, and we would take them back and forth. He spent most of his money in sending us to private schools so that we wouldn't fall behind, but not falling behind academically didn't mean not falling behind socially and psychologically. It was difficult for me because I could never plan for the future. I could never say *Next year I'm going to do this . . .* because next year I might be somewhere else. So yes. I think it was very hard for both of us, and I only see the value now, in retrospect, because I now understand that my internal life began then, when I started using books as an anchor and a way to understand the world, to feel connected to the world. I understood that I was intelligent, and my brother did too, maybe because our parents expected that from us. We knew that even though we didn't have what some of the other kids had, we had something else. That's not being arrogant. We just thought of ourselves as intelligent kids, and we didn't have to accept defeat. We didn't feel like victims; we knew that our lifestyle was special, that it was different. Of course we were rebellious when we entered our teens, but I don't think that we felt deprived so much as lonely.

Did you feel at home in both environments?

I don't know what at home means. I think I felt happier and more protected in Puerto Rico only because. . .what child doesn't like a house full of people? This was a time I describe in *Silent Dancing*, my creative non-fiction about those years. My grandmother was a dynamic, matriarchal, powerful force. She came from a family of eight brothers and sisters, but mainly I grew up in a woman's house. That's where, in the afternoons, I would hear the stories that are now part of my work. There was a tribe of cousins. One of Mama's daughters, my aunt, had her five children there because her husband had gone to New Jersey ahead of her. So it was my brother, me, five cousins What are you smiling at?

I'm smiling because it's a surprise and a pleasure to hear New Jersey, where I grew up, spoken of as a destination, a sort of exotic location people might want to go to.

But it *was*. So we had this tribe and it was wonderful. And then when we went to New Jersey, our lifestyle changed completely. My mother was very reclusive. I mean, you couldn't be in the streets in Paterson. Our father moved us away from the barrio as soon as possible. We lived in Jewish-owned buildings where he made friends with the Jewish men and their families, and I remember that he wanted us to be quiet, so that we wouldn't confirm the stereotype of the loud Puerto Rican. So from being wild in Mama's house, we went to walking around in our socks because Daddy didn't want our landlords to think we were loud. It was a constant shift back and forth between two cultures, two different ways of living. But I liked Paterson, and learned to love it in my own way. I went to a small high school with Italian and Irish kids, and the Catholic Church provided us a whole social realm.

What did that mean for you as children?

We were the "Catholic School kids." In Puerto Rico, every year I seemed more foreign to my classmates and to other people because English was becoming my first language and I was becoming "the little American girl." So even though I was one of two or three Puerto Ricans at St. Joseph's, I was still more at home there, when I got older, than I was in Puerto Rico. So my sense of home shifted, to answer the question that started all this. When I was quite small, being around my cousins and my family in Puerto Rico was secure and fun. When I was thirteen and fourteen and fifteen, I already had my own society in Paterson. I hated the move to Augusta at first. I believed that we were being transplanted to another world, and it took me some years to learn to love the South. But now I do.

Does that mean you now have three places that travel with you always?

(Laughter) Three cultures. Because the culture of Paterson, New Jersey is completely different from the culture of Augusta, Georgia. They might both be American cultures, but it was probably more of a traumatic shift from Paterson to Augusta than from Paterson to the island.

Do you think, looking back, that any of that dissonance you experienced resulted from your resistance to the move, rather than arising solely from cultural differences?

Probably. I mean, I didn't want to be here; but also I was not included. It was the first couple of years of the desegregation of the schools, and I went to a huge public high school that had, maybe, two black girls. I write about this in "Advanced Biology," where I say that people in Georgia seemed to come in two basic colors, black and blonde. There was no ethnic mix like there was in Paterson. And teenagers are *clique-ish*. I was not taken up by any group, so I became even more of a bookworm, and decided to get scholarships and spent all my time studying. I convinced myself that I wasn't attractive because I didn't look like anybody in the school. It's pitiful, but it's true. When a kid at age fifteen is different looking. . . . Just for example, say there is somebody from India, who in India might have seemed attractive, but in Augusta or Montana or whatever, the stranger loses the sense of how they look in their culture. In my own family, this was interesting. Two years after the move, my brother entered the same grade that I was in when we got here, and he was practically the Latin lover of the school. It was different then, more mixture had happened and he just didn't experience the alienation and sense of not belonging that I did.

When did all that change for you?

It all changed when I came to Augusta College. There were Ethiopians, and Asians . . . all sorts of people here, and so once again I found myself in a multi-ethnic situation. So basically, it was for those two years of high school that I felt I did not belong in any particular group.

How did you think of yourself then? As a Yankee? A Puerto Rican. . .?

Well, whenever the white girls at the high school would ask me *Where are you from?* I'd say *From Paterson.* And they'd look at me like *Well, that explains it.* (Laughter) To them, my just saying that explained my being different. But I thought of myself as a girl from Paterson. It's funny how your identity is formed, you know? Then when people started thinking of me as a Spanish girl, I started thinking, *Well yeah, that's right. That's me.* But I was just from Paterson. I mean, if you were in Clifton, New Jersey, and somebody said *Where are you from?* you said *From Paterson.*

(Laughter) Or Kearny, or Bayonne. You've said that books became your anchor, and every time you felt more fragmented you would delve deeper into books. How old were you when you started writing?

Oh! That was late. You have to understand that books to me were not just escapism; they were a realm I went to. I could be any-where and go into a book, and lose myself and be a part of some-thing else. I knew that I wanted to teach long before I knew I wanted to write, because I wanted to be around people who read books, and to continue reading books myself.

That sounds pretty straightforward.

Ah, but then I married at nineteen, had a child at twenty-one, struggled to get through graduate school and had little time for anything. I had a vague dissatisfaction not with anything I had, but with *what I didn't have.* I knew that there was something that I was missing in my life. When I would read poetry, I felt an intense desire to write poetry. Poetry triggered a need in me; one that can never be completely satisfied. And it still does. I still can't get through a whole book of poems without wanting to write one myself.

How do you know when you've read a really good poem?

Well, we could quote Emily Dickinson. . .

Ah, but I asked Judy Cofer. . .

I have the same organic response. First of all, sometimes I get to a line that hits me so hard that I have to stop right there. And sometimes I hold my breath. It's a physical response. I get goose-bumps. If I read something that is, you know, just amazing, it changes me physically. It is mysterious. It is an organic, living, sensory experience. And so when I read a poem that I love, I'm usually holding my breath, and I usually get goosebumps. My body responds to the words. A good poem is something that I treasure and go back to time and time again. There are, oh, half a dozen poems that I can't live without, and I have those always around me.

But you asked me when I started writing. I wrote a little essay about a particular time in my life. I was in my mid-twenties. I was finishing school. I had a child, a husband, and still I was saying What's wrong with me? I can't be having a midlife crisis! I'm only twenty-six. (Laughter)

And were you? Having a midlife crisis?

It was all the usual things. I felt I needed something but I didn't know what. Finally I said *Well, I'm a fool. What I need is to write poems.* I have these index cards that I kept from my thesis. Sometimes I'd turn them over and copy a few lines from a poem and then try my own. And I realized that what I needed was to write. I started writing these poems that I thought no one would ever look at, and I showed them to a colleague of mine, a friend, my first boss at Brevard Community College. She said *These are good! Work with them. Revise them.* And she told me about journals. I didn't even know about journals! And I didn't know about journals because I was immersed in my graduate studies. She told me about the *Georgia Review*, the *Southern Review. . .* , and I said *My God, there's a whole world of people out there, living writers.* And then I got hooked because I sent out a poem and the *New Mexico Humanities Review* took it. And that was it. I thought *I'm good enough!* (Laughter) Because someone else thought so. And of course that started the long haul of like fifteen rejections and one acceptance, ten rejections and one acceptance, eight rejections and one acceptance. So it took eight years of writing before I had enough poems to put into a tiny, tiny, slender book.

And that's the usual story with most poets. But poetry is my first love. Whatever else I'm doing, I'm working on poems.

What's the difference, as you experience it, between writing a prose piece (whether it's fiction or non-fiction) and writing a poem? What is that organic difference in the writing experience?

It's very different, I think, because poetry is very demanding. It's a discipline like no other. And you have to, or at least I do, get in a mode of deep analysis. When I'm writing a poem, hours have actually passed and I don't know it. It's almost as if I'm in a trance, but there's nothing mystical about it, nothing mystical about it at all. It is psychological, emotional, and physical, and it takes everything I have. Some mornings I have worked on a poem and felt like I had run three miles.

It's not that prose isn't demanding, but it's not demanding the same emotionally exhausting way. Poems have been defined, as Coleridge said, as the best words in the best order. That irritates my students because I always say that means that all the poems you ever want to write are in the unabridged dictionary. You just have to put them in the right order (laughter). But it's that right order, finding the best words in the best order. So I think of poetry as the ultimate discipline. I tell my students, *If you can write a successful poem, you can write a chapter.* The impulse for language is contained in that poem. I just had a fiction writer complain that poets can write novels, but novelists can't always write poems. It's hard to go in the other direction. So poetry is that extremely difficult, maybe ultimate, discipline.

With prose, even though it's very hard, I always have a sense of exploration and freedom. With poetry I have a sense of restraint, like I'm after that decorum and perfection. I may not achieve it, but I'm after it. In fiction I am trying to do the best thing, but it's like the difference between a trip to California when you have three days to get there and a trip to California when it doesn't matter when you get there. You can be exploring as you travel. You can take as long as you want. I hope that's an adequate image.

Well, you're making an important distinction, and you capture the sense of journey that so often goes with the best writing.

It's a different way of relating to language, not necessarily easier. It is very hard to write prose, but the feeling is different. So I approach the two differently as they do different things to me.

As someone who began writing as an adult, did you find that there were fairly immediate deep changes in your life?

Yes. Not overnight, but I went from the possibility of being bored with myself to the stress of having to write all the time. Since I started writing I have never been bored. The stress is in finding time. The world doesn't wait for you. It doesn't reward you. Until I learned to discipline myself and keep writing in my head even while I was doing other things, I was always feeling I've got to get back to this!. But after I learned to discipline myself to use the two hours I give myself from five to seven a.m., it became a peaceful sort of feeling, *Well, I will get to it in the morning. I will get to it tomorrow.* But even now, if too many days go by when I can't do that, I start feeling as if I've lost something very important.

That brings me to another question. Like many writers, I want to say female writers, you do many things. You teach at Athens, you do public speaking engagements, workshops, conferences, you're a wife. . .

Right. I travel between Athens and Louisville every week.

How do you negotiate all the, oh, magnetic hot spots in your life?

The short answer is like *How do you milk a canary? With great difficulty.* (Laughter). I don't know that it's managed. I have become a person of routines most of the time. Even though it sounds like I do a lot of disconnected things, my life is mapped out to include the things I have decided are important. Sometimes I give up a social life or free time in exchange for the life that I have. There are certain days during the week when I give myself totally over to my students and my teaching and my committee work. That's usually Monday through Thursday. But I still don't give them that two hours a day. They're mine. Every day starts with my work from five to seven. I do have to get my rest, so I have no social life during those days. If I go out, I have to be in by 9:30 or I'm useless the next day. Then on Thursdays I drive home to see my husband and do all the stuff that needs to be done at home, but I also bring my laptop. I don't really have a day off. I grade papers and I work. As far as the travel goes, I have to give up times that I would otherwise have free for writing or for leisure. Frequently I need to be at a conference and those are a lot of work. Those can be thirteen hour days. But still, I get to be with wonderful people and have the society of other writers and people who take writing seriously. So what do I need a social life for? (Laughter)

It sounds as if those occasions become your social life.

Well, it has become my world. I was working but I was still talking about the things that interest me most. After all, what do you do when you go out to a social luncheon? You talk about the things that interest you the most. Me, I happen to be this boring person who loves poetry and writing and literature more than anything. I have now come to terms with the fact that my social life and work life are the same, at least four days of the week.

That's a valuable realization.

Do you think so?

Don't you?

Well, it took me a while, because I used to say *Oh, if I'm writing, I won't be able to do this.* But now! You know, we're going on a family vacation to Puerto Rico. I'm taking my computer. People will sleep late and I'll have the mornings to work. Then the afternoons I'll spend with my family, but I will have put in four or five hours of work, because I want to.

Your most recent book is a reissue of Reaching for the Mainland, *which was originally published in 1987, with selected new poems. Would you read just the last part of "Letter from Home in Spanish" from the new poems? It's a marked contrast with the poems you selected for this book, because of the clear connection with Spanish.*

Of course:

"But, *basta*, enough for now."

I read her letter aloud, for the sound
of Spanish, and it becomes a *kyrie*,
a litany in a mass for the dead.
I take each vowel on my tongue.
La vieja brings tears to my eyes
like incense; *la muerte*
sticks in my throat like ashes.

Her blessing is a row of black crosses
on a white field.

It's clearer when you read the lines aloud, but even reading them silently, and having never studied Spanish myself, I get the strong lift of Spanish in the lines. How do you achieve that effect in English?

It is partly because Spanish was the language of my family, and I occasionally have spent entire days going back and forth and back and forth between the two languages. That could have resulted in 'Spanglish,' but with me it didn't because my parents were so vigilant about us speaking clearly in both languages. My mother spoke only in Spanish. My father spoke to us in English, but it was textbook English he learned from books. It wasn't that they were intellectuals. They were working people, but they wanted us to go to college. So they insisted on good grammar and that sort of thing. If I'm writing in English, the way that I use Spanish involves thinking in terms of syntactic usage and pronunciation within the sentence, so that the sentence both makes sense and has the right number of syllables. If the words are pronounced correctly, the right rhythms will come out of it; it is a stylistic and deliberate thing that I do. I did in *The Line of the Sun*, when I wanted to imply that the characters were thinking in Spanish. That's what I do in the poems too. I'm very conscious of English rhythms. I've become very aware of how the English works, which is very different from the way the Spanish works. It's tricky, but it's possible. Singer did it with Yiddish.

As a teacher, you went to the University of Georgia on a three year contract, went away, returned . . . and have now become a full professor. What do you see yourself doing at the university in, say, ten years?

That's a hard question. Our Creative Writing program is what I consider an emerging program. It's a very traditional department, and so we're having to work within certain structures. A couple of professors who started the program are retiring, and that leaves me as the senior person and two young people as assistant professors. So I don't know about ten years, but I think that for the next few years we'll be organizing this program, we'll be populating it with other writers. My job as I see it will be, first of all, teaching, which is what I want to do. And luring young writers from all over the country, and the best young professionals, to our program, so that maybe in ten years we'll be competitive with the best programs in the nation.

And what do you see as the 'right direction' for the program?

For one thing, a diversity of students. I'm not climbing onto the multicultural bandwagon; I think that's just silly. I've always felt this way. I feel that if we attract people from different parts of the country, different groups and so on, that will make it a vital, representative program. So I want to set out to do that, to bring more women, more minority groups but not at the expense of the high standards that we have. I want us to attract the best.

When you began writing in your twenties. . .

My late twenties. My students are twenty, twenty-one so that's a lot of time I lost. Most women have a story like that.

True enough. Many women writers of our generation seem to have come to writing later than the men, for what I think are pretty obvious reasons.

Yes. We had families and so forth.

Still, in your late twenties, having that first poem published gave you a sense of validation. In terms of years, it wasn't all that much later that you began getting relatively major recognition for your writing. How did that make you feel?

Well, it didn't seem all that fast to me. I guess it was four years after that first published poem that I got the grant from Florida. And then I went to Breadloaf, and that was a big deal for me. I met people there who have become my lifelong friends and mentors. It seemed to have happened quickly, but we're talking about 1978 close to twenty years ago. The overnight success has actually taken twenty years. So I saw it differently.

But you must have realized that it was a big jump from publishing a poem to getting a state grant.

Yes. It was. So I guess I have been more fortunate than many people that way. So I have to say that once I started working . . . . I remember a year after that first acceptance. I said to my husband, *If this one, which I think is my best poem so far, isn't accepted, I'm giving this up.* He reminds me of that. And I truly don't know that I would have, but I did say that as a sort of spell to myself to make a point. I am driven. From that time on, except for illness or other unusual circumstances, I have never missed a day of writing. So if the awards and everything else came after one hundred poems, by then I was writing every day. And there was the novel, which I started in the early eighties. It didn't come out till '89.

What drew you write that particular kind of story, the coming of age narrative?

The Line of the Sun? Well, it is a coming of age story, but it deals with very complex issues. It's used in women's studies and cultural studies, at all levels and in English classes. I think that *An Island Like You* is probably an adolescent or young adult's novel, because it stops at age fifteen. But I see *The Line of the Sun* as just a regular novel. It may seem like simple language but I attempted to address serious issues in the life of the Puerto Rican community. What drove me to write it was that I wanted to tell a story that couldn't be contained in a poem. I started writing a story, and it grew and it grew and it grew. It was hard to do. Many times I put it away. I didn't think that I could finish it. But after three and a half years of working on it every day, I did have a manuscript. It was the story itself that drove me, the story-telling impulse.

If you could go back in time, keeping all the knowledge that you have today, all the experience of building your identity as a writer, is there anything you would do differently?

I don't know. I always wanted to have a child and to teach and to write so it's not that I had an ideal life, but the minute I made a decision to write every day, I felt that I was doing what I needed to do, without sacrificing the other stuff. I think that I would now be really sorry if I had abandoned my family and left those things to go pursue art. I know that I would have written a lot more, many more, books if I didn't have all the other obligations, but I don't know that I would have done it differently. I think I would've just continued to pursue that rigid work schedule that I did pursue.

One distinctive aspect of your career has to do with ethnicity. Very often you are referred to, written about, introduced as, a Puerto Rican poet, or a Latina poet or writer. You're seen as a representative of Latino culture in America. Yet the poems you've selected for this book almost seem to avoid your Latina identification. They are poems about women named Hagar, Magdalene, Helen. . . .

Right. Penelope.

Why those poems specifically?

Well, often, because of the multicultural focus in the nation, what students and the public get to see of my work is representative of only one aspect of me. Of course, being a Latina is what I draw a lot of my material from, but I'm also a woman immersed in literature. My degrees are in English. When I started teaching world literature in English, I noticed that most of the women in those stories were silent. You know, just absent. They were spoken about, entered and left the room on quiet little feet, and I said, *Wait a minute. I want to hear what Hagar has to say about this, or Salomé, or any of the other women.* So I started writing poems to sort of give me the other side of the story that I wasn't able to give my students. They are persona poems, and so I thought this might be a good time to present work that would have more to do with my essential self, which is, I hope, a thinking woman.

And an angry one? If we go by these poems?

Well, they were actually done in anger not at men, or at one particular thing, but at the silence imposed on women. You know, I just worked with Tillie Olsen and she's still, forty-five years later, talking about those silences. I felt that these women would have been angry to know that they had come down through history as merely villains, or merely mothers. Each one of them had a complex life.

What particulars drew you to Hagar?

She is the mother of the dark son, the one that all of us dark people are supposed to be descended from. And she was used in a most abominable way, as a vessel. I have identified with her as the one who was silenced and told *We don't need you now. Leave. Disappear. We don't want your story around.* And yet she had mothered; she was the default wife. And so she was the dark, rejected mother. And so, one of the silent ones.

At the end of the poem you write of "the dark side of a covenant" rather than the *covenant.*

Right. A covenant is simply a promise. And these poems were written when I was finding out that I wasn't really going to get to teach world literature. I was going to get to teach male world literature. So they do show my resentment that even in the stories that supposedly feature women, they have silent roles.

Do you feel that has changed significantly in literature classes?

It has changed significantly by comparison with what we had before. I went through almost my whole graduate program, the first two years, without encountering any women writers besides Virginia Wolfe, and this was in the seventies! Occasionally we would have some other figures, oh, from Colonial America perhaps, but I didn't have many women professors and that may have been one of the reasons. I didn't really encounter even the Southern writers, like Eudora Welty and Flannery O'Connor until I took a course in Southern writers with a woman, taught by a woman. There are many more of us now, and I certainly include women writers in my classes.

To return to the poems, why Magdalene? Why not Mary and Martha, for instance?

I don't know. I guess I'm drawn to the outsider. I'm drawn to the woman we get sort of enticing glimpses of. I have to imagine what happened to Magdalene. I mean, we know that Mary was assumed into the sky (laughter), but Magdalene? What happened to her? In the presence of this most charismatic of men, she perhaps even *loved* him, does she look like one of these women that we see? Like Greta Garbo, haunted by a past that cannot be equalled? So I imagine her going around with dark circles under her eyes saying *Are you saved? Are you saved?* So I projected myself into this woman haunted by what could not be equalled. Maybe that's what artists are. We are haunted by what we think is perfection that we cannot reach.

Of course, art is a tricky word. It can mean almost anything to almost any number of people. The process of making art, though, can be talked about fairly concretely. When you were writing these poems, how did you know when a poem was done?

It was Paul Valery, I think, who said *You never finish a poem, you just abandon it.* I am a compulsive reviser, and I work and work and work. To me the poem is finished when I have put it under my control as much as I can, when I read each line and I know it is the best I can do even if it isn't the best that can be done. And then closure has something to do with when I come up with that line that speaks *The End* to me. Also, I focus on something that I want to say, and then I feel when I come to the end of that last line that I have said it the best that I can say it. With Hagar, the line came to me. And I said *The Bible begins and ends with covenants.* And so that line had to be the end of that poem. I wish that I could be clearer, but it's a sense of almost organic satisfaction, like having eaten your fill. How do you know when you're not hungry any more? You feel full. That's the way it is with poetry, with me.

Those closing lines force the reader to question too. It's a situation where the sound says closure and the sense says "Wait, what covenant?" or "Whose forgiveness, really?" or with Salomé, "But why must you dance?"

Or *Why don't you dance?* It's like, if you have to it may be a burden; but if you can't, it may be a burden of another sort. I seem to be attracted to the rejected ones. It's the rejected ones that need a voice, usually. In "Salomé". . . well, I find John the Baptist the most alluring figure in the New Testament, because he isn't Christ, but he knows he must speak for Christ. It's like being in the presence of a great poet. He was Christ's cousin, but he wasn't Christ. He intrigues me. So I have Salomé have an almost erotic connection to this man. Both of them have to perform. Salomé interested me, and I know that this poem has an erotic level. What if she desired him, but needed to make a decision for her own survival? Basically, she is having to go against her instincts in order to live. How many women have to do that?

And the dance? The dance is art. . .

Well, yes. I saw these women as creators, doers, makers.

They were silenced, in part, because they were dangerous?

Of course.

In "Judith" that seems to be reflected in her line about the dead Holofernes, "his blood covered us like a marriage canopy." Did you intend that as an indictment of the conventional ideal of the patriarchal marriage?

Absolutely. And here there's a murder involved. She is forced to seduce this man, and then use his own sword to kill him. I'm fascinated by the one Virginia Wolfe called the "angel in the house." Judith too is killing the angel in the house. I have a story called the "Maria Sabida Story," a folktale I translated, in which the woman conquers the assassin by marrying him. But then she has to sleep with one eye open for the rest of her life. So marrying the assassin, or killing your lover, is all part of the creative process.

In what sense, specifically?

I think that Maria Sabida, who was the smartest woman in the whole island according to the folk tale, knew that the only way to keep the killer from assassinating any more innocent ones was to marry him, to be with him at all times. But she also knew she had to sleep with one eye open, because he was, after all, an assassin. And I think many of us who give ourselves to art are like that woman who slept with one eye open because the assassin is the angel in the house, someone who claims to protect you and love you but is always trying to take away your time, who trades love for your time. So you either marry him, and when I say marry him I don't mean that it has to be a man, but that you accept what threatens you, so you can control it. It's like asking the tiger into your house and taming it, so that it is your guest rather than your enemy. As far as murdering your lover is concerned, in many ways you have to subjugate the passions that otherwise would rule your life, if you're going to have art. And I feel that many women also do that. I have been fighting the need to do that all my life because I want to be a mother, I want to have these things. It makes my life five times harder than those women who said I'm just going to write. I cannot divide myself in that way. To have love in your life when you're an artist is a sacrifice. It's a complex subject. I think Virginia Wolfe stated it very well when she said she was always trying to kill that solicitous creature, the angel in the house, so that she could get on with her business, writing.

I suppose that for our generation another face of the angel is the daughter who turned out "right," who was domestically competent, loving, lovely. . .

And put us in a bad light by comparison.

Penelope is relevant here. She married and had a son, but then her husband went away and she was left with only herself and her son. One likes to think that must have prompted a turning inward, a period of thinking about and re-ordering her priorities and her life. Did you intend her as an analogy for the artist who is a woman?

I saw her as an analogy for the artist, but also as the woman transforming herself into the artist. I had planned a long cycle of these poems, and then realized that I was going to be weaving and unweaving the shroud. I was always going to be writing about Penelope if I didn't just stop it. My poems, in the order that I conceived them, follow from Penelope seen as the lover of Odysseus, completely attuned to what he wanted and grief-stricken when he left, yearning for his physical presence; then poem by poem as she begins to discover things like the moth at her window and the trees outside and the revelers coming back. And she remembers that the bed that Odysseus made from the trunk of the tree, that she used to think of as a ship, is a ship that goes nowhere. In "The Drowned Sailor" she begins to discover a sense of the body and the self, developing an erotic life that's not strictly connected to Odysseus. In the last poem in the cycle, "Learning to Walk Alone," she actually leaves her castle in Ithaca where she has been slowly turning towards the outside world, and she follows her servant into a world of mangy dogs and flies and all that, but at least it's a living, breathing world. And of course her servant looks at her with great suspicion because the woman who is out in the world looks at the woman who is spoiled by wealth and kept and says *Why do you need to go out and work? You have luxury!* The poor women always see the women in their suburban houses as lucky. Think of Hestia, who was named after the Goddess of the hearth. She was supposedly the goddess none of the Gods wanted, so she had to stay by the hearth and keep the fire burning, since without a fire burning the gods didn't have a warm home to come to. Hestia leads Penelope to the outside world, but doesn't yet accept her. The working woman and the women of the upper classes have not come to terms yet in these poems. Hestia sees Penelope as the coddled woman with all the luck in the world, and of course Penelope has found that Hestia has the living, breathing world beyond the castle.

These poems are all very consciously literary. Emotional content notwithstanding, the poems work to declare themselves as part of the literary universe, with many literary reference points. Yet they also reflect much of what enriches your identifiably Latina work. Much of the recognition and concern with class differentiations among women echoes your own awareness of cultural outsideness and class difference as you experienced them growing up.

Yes, of course! My mother was the wife of a sailor, and she spent most of her life as a young woman waiting for her sailor to come home.

Or fearing him drowned. . . ?

Why yes. So this is not just about Penelope. It's about the women who are rejected and the others who are coddled into silence. The woman who seems to have everything but lacks real experience in the world, the woman whose life is nothing but work, who yearns for some of that luxury, and how we're all deluded into thinking that someone has what we need, when what we need is some kind of personal freedom that has nothing to do with rejected loved ones. It has to do with freeing our minds. It has to do with saying to my classes *I belong to the Emily Dickinson travel club, I stay home and see the world.* Someday I'll travel and see the world, but for right now nobody can stop me thinking and writing. I own my mind.

Which brings us back to sailing images again, sailors and ships and vanishing across the horizon . . .

And wives waiting. You know, it's the same old thing. We only have three or four ideas, and we rework them into different patterns of the weave.

And yet they don't get boring. Reworked they become more complex, more layered. For instance, there have been many fine poems about Helen of Troy, ranging from "the face that launched a thousand ships" to HD's poem in which Helen is only loved in Greece after she is safely dead. What do you bring to your Helen?

(Laughter) Tinted hair, looking her age in the morning. This came out of the old question *What do women want?* Somebody is always asking that, but this Helen says *All I ever wanted was one man's total attention.* It's a cynical poem in that, oh, she has Paris. And the whole world's attention is focused on her. She's accused of having started a war. But what does she want? She wants the men to stop plotting battles, everybody to just stop making a fuss and have one person pay attention to her. She doesn't want to be the cause of anything else. Of course I'm projecting this. I'm assuming that this is a universal feeling. I do think we have all felt that at some point, that it doesn't matter if nobody else listens, but that one person who's really important in our lives, we would like for that one person to pay attention, to understand our needs. To me Helen is a very sad figure.

When my husband read this poem, he looked at that phrase "one man's total attention" and said "As if that were a little thing."

(Laughter)

How would you respond to that?

I would say that is why I put it there. It is an immense thing. *One man's total attention.* And not just for ten seconds. For life. To have him always listen to what you need. That's what Helen didn't have. The men were plotting wars. They were doing this. They were doing that. We women have their attention for maybe a few brief months of their lives when their mating instinct is in full spate, but the rest of the time it's like *How do we compete here?*

When we see the story of Marilyn Monroe, we see that's what she went around craving. She didn't want millions of men's total attention. She wanted one man's total attention. And she died without getting it.

So the desired thing was ultimately unobtainable. One last question. How do you want the world to remember you when you're retired from public life, when you're not teaching any more, perhaps not publishing much though probably still writing. What do you want people to look at in your career and say "Yes, this is what matters. This is solid."

Having met Tillie Olsen I can probably say *What she has.* What shows in her mannerisms and her energy; that she feels that she said something, even if it was just one thing, that mattered to women, that was a wake-up call in some way. Wouldn't that be wonderful? To have written a book that makes someone, women or anyone say I didn't know this about myself until I read that book.

It's sort of like wanting one man's total attention. I'm not talking about a Nobel Prize winning book or whatever. I'm talking about something like *Silences*. To have something that needed to be said, and no one had said it quite that way before, and it changed a few lives. I would like that.

So if you're asking me to wish, that would be it. To be remembered for something that changed a few lives.

Hagar

For once,
let me tell my story first.
I knew Abraham without once
looking into his eyes.
The others warned me
of Sarah's anger
which could rise like the Nile
in its season.
But like the promise of a black cloud
over parched land, I was
the only hope of his shrinking body.
Heaven ignoring her pleas,
Sarah turned Sphinx eyes on me,
her handmaiden.
Bonded to silence
until I quickened with their need,
I dared to lift my eyes to heaven;
God laughed
and woke the dormant seed
in Sarah's womb.

After Isaac and the knife,
my son and I were cast out
into the desert night colder
than the eyes of the betrayer,
to keep the dark side of a covenant.

Magdalene, Years Later

"Are you saved?" Purple shadows
under her blazing eyes, hysteria

at the edge of her voice,
and everyone understands: she's mad.

Years later she preaches her gospel
of hair, wine, and oil

in the marketplace, still wearing
the faded robes of a courtesan.

The coins that the amused crowd throws
are the first stones she was promised.

For the price of a prayer
anyone can lose himself in her eyes;

the eyes that saw it all: the ritual kiss,
the trial, the cross. The eyes

that were blinded by the light of forgiveness.

Salomé

Did you love him? Like a fool
he poured out his life in handfuls
over the heads of the uncaring crowds.
Blinded by visions, he couldn't see
how you tried to bring him back
with your hands. Drawn by a melody
only he could hear, he stepped
straight into the pit. You wanted to understand
what drove him, so you looked inside his head,
only to find it dark as Herod's heart.
          Now,
at this late hour, you consider the thoughtful platter
you are holding aloft. Incongruously,
you imagine his face rising between your thighs.
Weary of men's rituals
you want to drop it and run. But the king
seems to be excited by the tinkling call
of the bells on your toes, he is clapping
for more wine, the music is playing,
and you must dance, Salomé.

Judith

You anointed me
with perfumed oil,
draped me
in the saffron robes
of a pagan whore,
and sent me
into the battle tent
to make history
with Holofernes.
All night I poured
the wine of your labor
into a gilded chalice,
and when he sank
deep into a dream,
I severed his head
with the sword
he had laid at my feet.
His blood covered us both
like a marriage canopy.

Morning in Troy

I rise early.
Morning light no longer flatters me. On the becalmed sea of our bed, he snores
gently, curled into himself like a contented infant.

I will quietly sprinkle cool water over my face, sweeten my breath
by chewing on a mint leaf, and brush the tangles
from my still luxuriant red hair, then return to his side.

All I ever wanted was one man's total attention.

Last night I cradled him between my breasts while that poor wretch,
Cassandra, wailed her prophecies of death by fire
up and down the streets of this strangely silent city.

      Knowing fear
is the antidote to passion, I got him drunk on wine and skin,
summoning Aphrodite to help me win this struggle.
And I did.

   Last night Troy slept while Paris burned.

from "Penelope's Journal"
Years Without News

"But I waste my heart away longing for Odysseus."
BOOK 19, THE ODYSSEY

Everyone treats me like a widow. Our son weeps alone
in his chamber, his eyes frightened like those of a fawn
abandoned in the forest. Servants whisper in the hallways.
        Thick currents
of sea-smells drift in through the windows of these rooms,
labyrinth of my sleepless nights. I sit very still listening
to our poet tune his lyre in the garden below. As the sun sets, he will turn his
eyes to our island's rocky shore.
        In the deepening pool
of nightfall, I chant a spell against sorrow, and brace myself,
knowing that in a moment of weakness my soul can be stolen
by a jealous god and dragged across the sky
like someone's wish.

Look at the sky for directions, Husband, but never
speak longingly of me.

from "Penelope's Journal"
The Drowned Sailor

When I first saw you break through
the wine-dark waters, your body
blocked the setting sun, an aureole
of light transforming you into a god.
        The tide rocked you,
spread your yellow hair crowned with seaweed,
opened and closed your limp hands, filling you,
emptying you, like a mother gone mad with grief
working over a dead child.
        I stood at the edge of the sea
until the sounds of the retreating waves,
like the suckling of an infant at the breast,
or of a man loving a woman's body, became one
with the rhythm of my breathing.
        Tonight you will travel
to Lord Poseidon's realm, down to that silent place
where there is no memory or desire,
only the slow melting of the flesh.

from "Penelope's Journal"
Learning to Walk Alone

Today I followed my servant, Hestia, down the dusty path
that leads away from the sea. Trudging toward
the barren hills that separate my house from her world,
her stiff back told me
that a woman walking home after a day of laboring
over someone else's hearth
had nothing to share with a fortunate fool
strolling in the heat of late afternoon
for pleasure.
    As we approached the last clump of trees
huddled together like beggars at the edge of the village,
I gave up the contest of wills. I followed Hestia's brown form
with my eyes, as she descended into a marketplace
filled with hagglers, stray dogs, and flies until
she became part of the crowd.

    I stood there with my arms around a thin old tree
for a long time, listening to the sounds of words
I could not decipher, the empty cadences of far-away voices
rising and falling

        Without you, Odysseus,
I have come to hate living on this island, this constant whine
of the sea licking its own wounds. If I could I would follow
the vagrant fools to crowded places and feast on crumbs.
I would wait with the patience of birds
for someone to extend an open hand.

from "Penelope's Journal"
Dear Odysseus

This morning a lark entered my chamber
alighting on the lowest branch of a tree
that is our marriage bed. He sang for me.
At daybreak, I heard chanting and laughter
in the distance. It was a crowd of young worshippers
welcoming spring, walking home
from the fields they had blessed with wine,
songs, and lovemaking. The girls walked arm-in-arm
ahead of the young men whose eyes were fixed
on their graceful bodies like mariners
first sighting land.
     When you came for me,
we walked on my father's fields, and you said
green was not the color of your destiny. The sea
was calling you even then. Bird song and nursing calf
amused but did not hold you, the mystery
of earth-grown things, the passing
of Apollo's chariot were matters for the minds
of lesser men, you said.
     Stars enticed you
for their coded messages, Odysseus, the moon
was a torch held over the chart of the night sky,
so you, forever captain, could plot
your next destination.
     I have begun
to see things more clearly, as if my eyes were stronger
from willing your ship to appear on the horizon.
On the ledge of a window facing the setting sun,

I found a moth with nearly invisible wings
I wished into flight. I watched a leaf
leap down from the branch of a tall tree
to ride the gathering wind.

35

    I wait for clouds,
moving slowly as wounded soldiers, to bring me
the smell of rain, a distant promise I take in
in deep breaths.

from "Penelope's Journal"
Penelope

Odysseus, the moon
looms over our house, its face split
in mockery of my grief. I have
seen it change expressions six times
since you left: Half a year ago
you last made love to me
on the lap of this old tree you carved
into our marriage bed. The branches
you said were the fingers of gods
blessing our union now seem to threaten,
their shadows fall across my body
one by one with the movement of the moon.

    Before your journey
you took me to your ship. Together we watched
your men raise the sails. Flapping in the good wind,
they were the wings of a great white bird
you held captive to move your ship with its desire
for flight. To the sounds of its struggle
we came together in your cabin. In the dimness
of this man-place you promised me with a thousand kisses
that you would return, Odysseus.

    A sudden gust
has swollen the canopy of our bed
like the sails of ship. My ship, Odysseus,
a ship that goes nowhere.

Toi Derricotte

Peeling Back Experience

Born in Detroit, Michigan, Toi Derricotte has published three collections of poetry, Natural Birth *(Crossing Press, 1983),* The Empress of the Death House *(Lotus Press, 1978) and most recently* Captivity *(University of Pittsburgh Press, 1989) which is in its fourth printing,* The Black Notebooks *(W.W. Norton & Co., 1997) and* Tender *(University of Pittsburgh Press, 1997). Of* Natural Birth, *Adrienne Rich has said: "Her words touch the reader as life has touched her, soul and body. This is a strong, sensuous, original, courageous book."*

Among her many honors and awards, Derricotte is the recipient of two fellowships from the National Endowment for the Arts (1985 and 1990) as well as the recipient of the United Black Artists, USA, Inc., Distinguished Pioneering of the Arts Award (1993), the Lucille Medwick Memorial Award from The Poetry Society of America (1985), a Pushcart Prize (1989), and the Folger Shakespeare Library Poetry Book Award (1990). Her poems have appeared in many magazines, including *American Poetry Review*, *The Iowa Review*, *Callaloo*, *The Paris Review*, *Ploughshares*, *The Kenyon Review*, *Massachusetts Review*, and in numerous anthologies, including *The Pittsburgh Book of Contemporary American Poetry*, *A New Geography of Poets*, and *New American Poets of the 90's*. She has read and given lectures at colleges, universities, libraries, museums, theaters, and bookstores throughout the world.

She is an Assistant Professor in the English Department of the University of Pittsburgh, and she has taught in the graduate creative writing programs at New York University, George Mason University, and Old Dominion University. She founded with Cornelius Eady, in 1996, Cave Canem, a workshop retreat for African-American poets.

Derricotte was born Antoinette Webster on April 12, 1941, daughter of Benjamin Sweeney Webster and Antonia Webster (nee Banquet). Describing her family's situation in life, Derricotte relates, is complicated, something that "would take a book to explain." Looking back, she today recalls a childhood to some extent dominated by her Roman Catholic education. She attended a Catholic grade school, Holy Rosary, and an all girls Catholic high school, Girls' Catholic Central, from which she graduated in 1959. She recalls, as the worst experience of her grade school years, being accused by a teacher of changing another girl's answer on a test. As Derricotte remembers the incident, "I didn't think I had done it, but after she questioned me and wouldn't believe me, I wasn't sure." Her favorite memory from the same period is an occasion when a cousin surprised her, on a visit to Chicago, with "a trip to a stable and a beautiful horse ride." As an adolescent, Derricotte relates, her parents' divorce "was both the best and the worst thing" to happen to her.

After graduation from Girls' Catholic Central, she attended Marygrove College for one year, then Montieth College at Wayne State University, graduating in 1965. She completed her M.A. at New York University in 1984. Her 1960 marriage to artist Clarence Reese ended in divorce in 1964, and she is presently separated from Bruce Derricotte, whom she married in 1968. Her son Anthony (Tony) was born in 1962.

Although Derricotte has worked in a number of occupations, ranging from the Manpower program in Detroit through public school teaching of the mentally and emotionally retarded, to her present position as an assistant professor of English, when asked for her occupation she responds "Profeminist Poet" without hesitation. Of all the experiences that have made up her life, she relates that the one thing that has marked her most deeply as a woman and a poet is "My mother's sadness, my mother's sadness, my mother's sadness." Her hope for the future, she says, is to "keep writing about personal experiences and sometimes burst out with joy poems."

As part of a generation that grew up on Allen Ginsberg and his peers, I have to ask what prompted the line in Allen Ginsberg" that reads "miracle laden Christ with electric atom juice."

That's an interesting line. He talks about a game that he used to play. I don't know whether he used to play it with other writers of the Beat Generation, or if he just made up this phrase to talk about what he tries to do when he writes poetry, but it's called "hydrogen juke box." What he meant, as far as I can remember, is that you try to put words together so there's a blank spot in the middle. The mind of the reader has to leap across with a kind of energy that makes the connection. It makes a kind of electric connection because the mind has to leap over something that wasn't there. So a lot of times the reader gets a surprising way of putting ideas together, always feeling a tension and a need to construct an image without a remembered image to refer to. So in a way, the act of reading becomes an act of creating one's images. That's how I got the line. You know, everyone who reads that poem—well, not everyone but many people—come to me afterwards with an Allen Ginsberg story.

I guess he's become part of a mythic substratum in the world of twentieth-century letters.

Yes. I saw him, after he had Bell's palsy and after his heart attack. It's frightening, but the generation that produced *Howl* is gone — or at least is going. . . . And it really is frightening. Because what do we have now to replace it? That's a big question.

Do you have an answer?

I was thinking about how complicated one's emotions are about so many things. On one level, *Howl*. . . and *Kaddish! Kaddish* influenced me so much! If you read *Kaddish* and then read *Natural Birth*, you'll see that in my subconscious mind, although I didn't write *Natural Birth* until seventeen years after my son was born and probably twenty years after I read *Kaddish*, *Kaddish* was there. To me it was the possibility of using prose — of writing prose that was poetry and making a narrative and making it a book and dedicating it to a person that one has very conflicted feelings about — his to his mother, mine to my son — a kind of monument to the fallible and yet in a way most beautiful love. The possibility of creating this perfect kind of gift, which is a work of art. All these things were in my mind during those years I struggled with my own shame about giving birth to my son in a home for unwed mothers. There's an institutional connection too. There's a wonderful part in *Kaddish* where Ginsberg, at twelve years old, had to take his mother to Greystone, which was a mental hospital. And at twelve years old, he was the one who took his mother on a Greyhound bus and committed her. And I gave birth to my son in a "home for unwed mothers." I don't even know if those things exist nowadays. So you see there was a sense of me not only idealizing what came from that generation — and me going to the cafes, listening to jazz and feeling like I was an artist, that romantic placement of the self inside some kind of idea of what a culture is. But there was also the other part of that. Where were the women? Where were the black people? How would Ginsberg regard me?

An impressive series of questions.

Some of my greatest difficulties have been with how to relate emotionally to those men whose work meant so much to me, but I'm afraid someone like me might not mean so much to them. So if you ask, where is literature, or what's next or what's now. . .hopefully what's now is my voice and the voices of some people who might not have been able to speak because they were repressed, feeling ashamed and unimportant, and the culture they were part of supported that. Maybe some of those people will have a chance.

Let us hope! You've just opened up a whole vista of questions I'd like to explore. They have to do with Natural Birth *and then with* Captivity, *which is a vastly different book in many ways. Just for example, reading* Natural Birth *(especially in light of this conversation) I can hear the echoes of* Kaddish *(the Ginsberg stance, the Ginsberg line) but changed. And yet as I read* Captivity, *I don't get those echoes at all. "Allen Ginsberg" is a moving, ambivalent tribute but it doesn't read like Ginsberg any more. Somewhere between those two books, something happened to you as a poet. Can you explain a little about what that is?*

Yeah. Something happened and something continues to happen to me as a poet but it's not an easy thing for me to speak about the styles in my writing, because I don't understand it all.

Still, your recent work seems to have a serenity that I didn't sense in your earlier work, a suggestion of realized strength rather than a voice still trying to consolidate itself.

Art is such a liar! You make something and you make it to express the truth. At least for me, art and truth are very connected, like finding a way to clarify the deepest truth. But in some way what I create in my art may not be exactly what I am feeling in creating it.

In other words, the serenity in the poem isn't necessarily your personal serenity when you write.

Um-hum. Matisse said that the artist has to turn himself inside out before he dies. I think that voice is not something that one attains or arrives at. I think voice is like layers that you peel. It's one of the reasons why art is a constant challenge. It's like the river of running water. You put your cup in and there's always something new. In my case, I'm constantly changing. What I notice constantly changes. What I'm trying to incorporate in my work constantly changes. Form to me is always a question mark. I think that in *Natural Birth* and in the poems I'm writing now there's more of a prosaic feel to things, maybe more Whitman- or more *Howl-* or more *Kaddish*-like. But who knows why? Williams talks about the breath line . . . it's very mysterious to me why anyone writes in a certain style and why some writers are recognizable for that one style for their whole careers. I don't know if I'd be recognizable for that reason. I don't know if you were to read *Natural Birth* and then to read *Captivity* you'd know from the style that it was me. You might know by context, or by a certain kind of deep image that is the same, or a certain kind of need that's the same. But in some ways I find that I'm constantly demanding of my work that I struggle. I feel that if I know what I'm doing, I'm not creating any more. In the back of my mind, always, is *Don't get comfortable*. Don't get comfortable.

And this is consistent?

I don't know how many times it has happened to me that as soon as I know what I'm doing it all falls apart and I go through a period of re-establishing what a whole work is. For me that's what a book is, a way of re-establishing the balance and relationship between ideas and coming up with a kind of central idea that holds everything together. But every time I do a book it's a different kind of main idea. I have to find out what that is before I can put the book together.

That makes sense if voice and form are constantly evolving, and constantly being "unlayered"—but it's at odds with the poet who might say "It took me years to find my line"—or "my stanza."

I don't think that'll ever happen to me. Maybe it will. Maybe I just still haven't gotten to that point, but everything changes all the time and I think there are some qualities in my voice that I like better than other qualities, and gee, I wish I could write certain kinds of poems all the time, but I take what I can get.

If you could write them all the time, wouldn't you be suspicious? Think about that problem of ease. When it gets comfortable, when it gets easy, then according to what you said a little earlier, something's wrong. You can't trust it.

I guess that's part of my makeup. I'm very hard on myself. I'm very scrupulous about things. I agonize about little things that people probably think are like, *Well, okay, that happened. So what?* I agonize about relationships and little things that happen between people, in the same way I agonize about art. If it's too simple, somehow I'm not listening to the complexity of it. That's just part of my style, I guess.

You said earlier that you wrote Natural Birth *seventeen years after the birth of your son. Do you know why it took that long for you to get to write it? Or why that was the right time for it?*

Well, locusts have a seventeen year cycle. They're underground for seventeen years before they emerge. I think of a book like that. I think there's a natural cycle or rhythm to the mind. I'm not sure how that's changed by the way we exchange information now. I mean, think of the talk shows. Two weeks after your child is abducted, you're on *Oprah* talking about how you felt. You get a certain kind of information and you get a certain kind of release of the kinds of tension in the situation that perhaps didn't used to get released in this way. So maybe things are changing, right now, in terms of what I think of as a natural cycle, but I have noticed that lots of times people don't write about experiences that deeply changed them until seventeen, twenty years later. Think about Vietnam. Think about how so many women say, after the birth of their children, Oh, I don't remember what happened. I forgot everything. There's some way that we're protected, because our poor little frail minds can't know too much until we're able to sustain what we've already learned and something inside of us changes. We get more distance from the experience; there's a feeling of safety. Circumstances change so that we feel more, maybe, in control. More able to look at the complexity of what happened after time has passed. I think about men writing about killing people in Vietnam, their guilt, the responsibility they feel . . . There are things that you can't tell immediately after, and maybe can't even consciously know. So these are the kinds of things that take many, many years to come to the surface. I'm not sure how *The Oprah Winfrey Show* is going to change that. Maybe the same patterns will exist in the future, so artists will still wait or take that long to really write about what it feels like when their child is abducted. Or maybe art will change dramatically as a result of this happening in our culture, the way the computer changes the process as one writes, or e-mail. You know, Louis Simpson says that you can't write a poem unless the pen it comes from is in your hand, because the poem is organic and it comes from your body, and if you're not using your actual hand to hold a pencil, you're not going to get the kind of organic form. . .you don't get that from a computer or a typewriter.

My impulse is to take that, in a larger context, to mean that Louis Simpson can't write a poem on a typewriter or a computer, but that other folks can. And do. And need to!

Right. But the question is are you going to be able to look at it and tell whether the poem is written by hand or with a typewriter. Are you going to be able to tell the kind of consciousness that's embodied — in maybe a different kind of form. Will somebody writing on a computer go for the bottom of the page? as opposed to having a feeling of a core inside the middle of the poem, like the perfect room shaped little HD poem. You know?

(Laughter) I always wondered how she did that. Composing on computer has become crucial to me because I see the printed line as I write the poem . . .it's nothing at all like the ballpoint and legal pad days. Does that bring us back to evolution of form and voice?

Yeah! Yeah! It really does.

There's a poem in Captivity *that has very close ties to* Natural Birth *in some ways. It's titled "A Note on my Son's Face." It's brutally honest without ever losing its lyrical quality. How much time elapsed between this poem being written and* Natural Birth *being written?*

Oh God, I think about eight or nine years. Maybe even ten years.

That's a long time. It really extends that natural cycle you mentioned a great deal, and offers more layers of the same experience since it seems to be a poem to your grandson as well as to your son, and maybe even more than that, a poem to yourself. . ." I wanted that face to die,/to be reborn in the face of a white child." and "Did I bend over his nose/ and straighten it with my fingers/ like a vine growing the wrong way?/ Did he feel my hand in malice?"

One thing is the way that mothers — all mothers I think — wonder if their own limits and problems and ambivalence and actions and lack of actions have harmed their children. It's a question we have about that relationship. Some people say that when your child is born you pick up a bag of guilt that you carry for the rest of your life. So there is that in it. But I think that in particular I'm always trying to, oh, deconstruct people, deconstruct family — in a way taking apart the ideal, the thing that we're given, the most common and easy reference. The cultural reference. In that poem, I'm addressing so many things . . . like the idea of the strong, perfect, black mother. It's been providing positive images of black women, and their strength. It's been a way to deal with the negative stereotypes that black women have had to deal with — that they were animals . . . all this from slavery. . . that they were sexual animals and responsible for their own rape. So there were a lot of ways in which this "positive" image of strong black women also wiped out parts of our identity, the more complex ways in which race, racism, affected our family life and the ways in which we loved each other. There was an idea during the fifties that if you just got your house in the suburbs, and put Spot, Dick, Jane, Mother or whatever in the house . . . then everything would be peachy. There was this ideal, this false ideal, behind our images of who we are. Some way it's replaying in the back of our minds all the time and we're judging ourselves. So as a black woman, in some way, I'm judging myself the way a white woman would because I've absorbed the same image of the suburbs and the little perfect life with the picket fence. And there's a part of me that thinks I've failed when I put myself up against this false ideal. But what is missing is that there are a lot of truths, a lot of experiences, a lot of events, that have become masked, hidden — because we're shamed. Or we feel that to reveal these things would be destructive, and I understand that, because when it's taken for granted that you're inferior, that you're an animal, then part of the question of survival has to do with presenting a certain image of yourself in a "positive" way. It was a kind of protection for the people of the race to survive, to go forward, to get some things, to get money, to get an education . . . whatever. I'm trying to say that these "positive" images served racism as well as other points of reference, because it's very good for people who live within it and accept racism as part of their daily existence. So to read about all these strong black women who have survived and their children — and they were perfect mothers — is a way of saying racism isn't really destructive because individuals, if they're just strong enough, if they just work hard enough as individuals, can overcome it. Do you understand what I'm saying?

Yes. You're saying that even positive stereotypes can be destructive to those they portray.

Those positive images serve us, black people, because we need positive images — to feed us, to give us ideals — but we also need them as a protection against the stereotypes that have been foisted on us. Right now I'm reading in newspapers and articles that if you present ideas that are too complicated, you don't get funded, because the people in power, who happen to be white folks in this country, don't want ideas to be too complicated. Give us anguish or give us joy. Please don't give us both at once. What I want to do is make a room within the ideal for what feels more authentic as a description of love in very terrifying times, threatening times. Times that are threatening to the mother, to the ego of the mother. How does the mother love the child? What is love really like when people are frightened and threatened and struggling for their own ego survival? I think that's important because I think love really exists between people. I felt it in my own family — terrifying love sometimes, complicated love, a love you don't want, a love you run away from — but something there that's authentic. I'm trying to get closer and closer because I believe in it. The only love we really have is that complicated love.

That's a courageous thing to try to make room for, I want to say 'on paper,' but maybe it would be more accurate to say "in the poetic line" or even "in life." In the final section of "A Note . . ." you deliberately work in the context of that "complicated love," and in a specific racial context, but the third section, taken alone, is almost apocalyptic, particularly the last two lines, "The worst is true./ Everything you did not want to know."

Right. It's not just black folk. What I'm trying to say in that third part is that you can't work with circumstances unless you face the blood on your own hands. Those people who try to leap over their own bloody hands, and those countries, and those pockets where we band together in an effort to deny our own complicity in things as they are. . . . It can't work. Part of my work is making myself become conscious of my complicity in the devastating forces that are a part of our culture. Part of that for me is that consciousness is a profoundly altering event in one's life, one's emotional and psychological life. Being conscious is a very painful thing, a very difficult thing, and if one thinks that one becomes conscious, and that therefore things become easy, as I once thought. . . . I did. I thought *If I write this, and I'm conscious of it, then the problem's going to go away. I'm not going to suffer any more about it.* It's not true. Consciousness does not make the problem go away. This is part of the reason why race stuff is so difficult, because people think *Oh, we'll admit to each other that we have these complicated feelings and then we'll be friends* (chuckle) *and get along.* The problem is you don't become friends and get along. Sometimes things get rougher after you become conscious and speak about your consciousness. You have to be extremely motivated to be conscious, because it is painful. For me, art is the motivation. Creating art, making something that has clarity and beauty that's lasting, is my motive. It's the drive that pushes me through the pain of experience. But I know it's not going to make things easier. It's going to make things harder. But the hope I have — and I think this happens for me — is that my own consciousness in some way shapes my ability to control the kinds of relations I have with other people so that perhaps I don't take that pain and use it to hurt another person quite as easily as I would if I wasn't conscious. So I think consciousness can actually be a saving grace — that with consciousness we're not as likely to hurt others as without. You hold the pain inside and understand it's part of the pain of being human without projecting it and taking it out on others.

That points to your experience at an artists' colony, which as you've spoken about it elsewhere, seems to have been a mix of conscious and unconscious — 'irritation' is probably not a strong enough word, 'malice' may be too strong — but fierce discomfort. It seems as if most of what you've written about that has tended toward prose rather than verse. Is this an accurate perception?

(Laughter) I don't know. I don't know if it is prose. I don't know if it is verse. I guess I don't know both! People come up to me after a reading and say *I liked that poem about such and such,*—and I've written *The Black Notebooks* with the same kind of intensity and consciousness of form as I have for any poem. It's just that it's shaped like boxes, instead of like, oh, like . . .

A poem? With lovely, large white margins?

Yeah. But now that I think about it, you look at the white space on the page and you look at the black space on the page, and you get a sense of a poem even before you read it. You're looking at it as if it's hanging in space, and what does the space around it say to you? With *The Black Notebooks*, now that I think about it, the text is shaped like boxes, the way that houses are shaped like boxes. Maybe there's a way in which these box-like shapes are a kind of emotional complexity that I couldn't hold in a more commonly-recognized-as-poem line. So it looks like prose, it feels like prose in a certain kind of way, it has the same deliberateness . . .

Does it also have the deliberate use of form that poetry has?

Absolutely. And there's clarity I struggled for in syntax, in language, in emotional compression, leaving out everything that wasn't absolutely necessary just as I would with a line of poetry — that way you kind of up the power with every word, you hope, and every line. That kind of tension. And that's why *The Black Notebooks* has taken me twenty years to write, and why it's 200 pages, and not the several thousand more that I wrote.

That's a lot of hard work.

It *is* a lot of hard work. And you have to be really motivated to do the hard work of creating art, and who knows why some people are motivated and some people are not? There were people I studied with when I first started taking poetry classes, who appeared to be a lot more talented than I was. One friend of mine who was a wonderful poet when she was starting out — brilliant, instantly. She went on to become a baker (laughter) and she loves it. And you have to love a thing to do it — and that's all very mysterious!

Well, talent is mysterious. How would you define it?

You wonder, is it love? I tried to draw when I was young. I had a great desire to draw — but it turned out that drawing was only a precursor to my learning language and making images. I wish I could've been a singer. When I hear these wonderful singers, I think Oh God! If only my words could leap up like that — I guess you have to find what you do the best, then work at it real hard.

So the thing that you do the best is actually your talent, and the work is what validates it?

Yeah. Can we backtrack? I loved what you said about malice and irritation — because it seemed to me that it was their malice and my irritation. Or my irritation and my rage.

Were you able to allow yourself rage at the time?

Absolutely not. Again, the whole thing about the evolving condition of consciousness, one's response when one is threatened. If you're in an environment where you feel you're tolerated, or sort of put there not because of who you are but because you fill a quota. . . . The day I arrived at the artists' colony, a black person left; on the day I left another black person arrived.

That's unnerving at the least.

But that's the way it is. There's this whole idea that because you're an artist you're removed from the sins of your fathers, that in some way you've escaped. . . . And it's such an ego trip because we're all just human. Think what it's like when you read a poem by Ezra Pound, and you love this poem and then you suddenly remember this guy was an anti-Semite, or when you read some of the work by writers that you adore and you find out they hated black people. Again, how does this affect your feeling for them, your feeling for yourself, your feeling for the work, for what you write about? Certainly, when I went to this colony — these things were not revealed all at once to me. So that when I saw a black person leave on the day I arrived I was hoping that a black person wouldn't come on the day I left. . . but that meant I had to kind of keep that in the back of my mind for six weeks — which didn't make me feel perfectly comfortable all the time. So it was a question of how does one contain these things, these emotions, and still relate to people? Love people and still admit one's complicated feelings?

So, in this kind of situation does one simply squash those feelings?

Yeah. You do. I did. I was a practice case. Was I going to do well there, or was I going to be a pain in the behind?

And would anyone know that you were really there anyway? Were you recognized as a black person? Or were you perceived as someone who was not "quite" black or "really" black?

Well, there are all kinds of responses to finding out I'm black—from white people and from black people too. Sometimes it's *I knew you were black all along.* Reality's not reality. When you throw racism in, you can't know what anyone is perceiving, because racism twists everything so you don't know what the truth is. There is a postponement of understanding a truth that happens when I come and I see a black person leave on the day I come, and then I have to postpone understanding of whether this is part of the process here — am I just somebody who fits in for six weeks here, and then they have another person to fit in the slot? I have to postpone my understanding of the nature of reality in a way. I think that racism causes this kind of postponement. And in a way, it's kind of a good thing for an artist, but it's not an easy thing. *Is this part of what people seek in art?* One of the things readers look to women and writers from multi-ethnic backgrounds for is the kind of experience that double consciousness has brought about. In a way, when you're a quota "outsider," you're looking at the same things that somebody's looking at who's not an outsider, but you see it in a more alive or complicated way and it helps. It's one of the reasons people are buying a lot of books by women and by ethnic writers. There's some way in which it enables the reader to see reality in a more complicated way. I went to a reading a few weeks ago by Barry Lopez, who goes to a lot of strange environments and writes about surviving in them. An interesting thing is that when you go into a "strange" environment, you see things because your mind is just awake in a certain kind of way, the way a writer's mind is supposed to be awake all the time. I think that's what double consciousness is, in a way — you know, the W.E.B. Du Bois idea that if you're black in America you see things both through your eyes and the eyes of the white culture, because you have to see things both ways in order to survive. I think that kind of double vision is really a kind of awareness that allows you to experience reality in an alert and alive kind of way. When you're comfortable, you just don't see things. You don't see what's really true. In a way, I think that double consciousness is a really good thing for artists to have.

Do you think art, with it's reliance on double consciousness, has any hope of changing things?

I don't know. I just don't know. I say at the end of one of the pieces I wrote recently that we're all part of a complicated web that's holding us up. We each have a part to play that's an important part. I can't feel that art has some messianic role in the redemption of humanity, but it may. That's the kind of energy I put into my work, as if it could do something really important, and really change the way people relate to others — not to hurt others so readily and easily and without thought. I mean, as you said about the artists' colony, the things people did could be described as being "with malice" or just "non-thinking." The whole idea of people doing things and then saying Well, you know, everybody says that. Like at one time, if you said *Don't call me honey* . . . men might say Oh, *I mean it as a compliment.* I'm going a little off the track now, but yeah. I'm trying hard to make a change in how people think about the subtle things that go on in interactions. The subtle things that are communicated. For people to just know that there's a certain kind of vulnerability that all of us have, and for people to be conscious of that . . . .

And now we're back to the problem of consciousness again — of people being fully awake . . .

Maybe it's a kind of meditation — being awake in that way. Writing is a form of meditation too . . .

A very muscular sort of meditation.

Yes, it is. But it's still the same kind of attention to the present moment. Or maybe bringing the mind to bear, to recognize what's actually going on right now, in the moment. That's a kind of meditation. There are all kinds of meditation. Buddha said *Meditate as if your brow is on fire.* There are meditations where you move. You know, I think it's important to bring these awarenesses into our writing programs and even into our own practice of writing, but sometimes when I have worked with people and done relaxation exercises — and I know this sounds hokey to many of us who are accustomed to the Iowa style of workshop, where you come in and tear a poem apart, and that's what a workshop is. So it's hard for some of us to bring in what you might think of as new age techniques, but I have found that when I do relaxation exercises with kids, when I go in to teach poetry in a school program, and when I work with adults, that they really do access, in a more free way, a lot of language — if you want to just talk about technical aspects. I'm not just talking about spilling their guts. I'm talking about the quality of language that is more intense and more unique and varied. So I think it's a very good thing to remember that the poem is centered in the body and comes from the body.

When you were growing up, did you have any idea at all that you were a poet?

When I was about twelve, I started thinking that maybe . . . But there was a real conflict, of course, because if you're a black, middle class girl, you're either going to become a doctor. . .

Or a teacher?

That's right! But you *weren't* going to be a poet. It seems to me that if you were middle class, certain kinds of associations didn't exist. Now I'm trying to think of who were the people in Detroit that became poets, where did they come from. I mean black people. I mean what neighborhoods did they come from. I have to think about this. This would be interesting for me to do. You know that Cornelius Eady and I are doing a workshop for African-American poets — *Cave Canem.* This is the first year, and we've got so many wonderful applicants from all over the country — so many established African-American poets who want to come read and spend a day with us. I mean we can't pay anybody, we're not making any money ourselves — we're just doing this.

People are not paying tuition. We did not want to begin this whole thing of scholarships and fellowships and this way in which hierarchies are created. We've experienced how damaging that is. But people want to come because of so many experiences that African-Americans have had that are like the one I talk about at the artists' colony — where you are the only one, where there are all these pressures. And as you say, I'm not always recognized as black.

That's really almost a double layer of alienation that's imposed on you. As if the unconscious people meeting you (keeping in mind what you've said about consciousness) are perceiving you as white, or maybe some other ethnicity that they perceive as not "quite" white, so that you're being pressured to respond to them in a way that denies your ethnicity, but at the same time forces you to internalize your ethnicity in what could easily be negative ways.

Yeah. I don't know what people see when they see me. That would be interesting to find out, but difficult. As long as racism exists, one doesn't know the veracity of even what people report.

It gets very convoluted doesn't it?

Oh yeah! Like for example, I had my best girlfriends over to dinner when my mother was in town visiting. And they're black women and after she went upstairs we started talking about color, and I said *Well, you know, my mother's much lighter. She looks more white than me.* And they said *Oh no, you look more white than her.* And then I have to think, well why did I see my mother that way all my life? Or has she changed? Have I changed? And my girlfriends have an investment in assuring me that *Oh Toi, don't worry, you look black.*

It sounds as if everyone wants to tell you that you look the way they think you want to look.

Yeah. That could be part of what's going on here too. How is one to know, as long as racism exists, what is real? It changes things. I've had very dark people come up to me after a reading and say

Oh, I know what you're going through because people always think I'm white. And then I have to say, *Well, maybe people do think they're white. Maybe something's wrong with the way I'm seeing them.* Or is the person saying this out of wanting so badly to appear white that it becomes possible to deny the actual way their face looks? This is the kind of complexity that racism throws in, because of the pain of what it means to be black. There's a book by Andrew Hacker called *Two Nations: Separate, Hostile, and Unequal.* He talks about an experiment that he did where he went to a college and asked a random sample of college kids *Okay. Everything about you stays the same, same mother, father, home, income job. . . but we just change the color of your skin and make you black. How much do we have to recompense you for the change?* The typical answer is *$1,000,000.00 a year for the rest of my life.* So on some deep level we do know what it means to be black, and we know that it profoundly changes access and relations and meanings and empowerment. All those things. So yeah, it makes reality very shifty.

And very masked. You spoke earlier about the element of masking, which also figures in "Christmas Eve, My Mother Dressing," when the mother in the poem is putting on her makeup, "as if we never would have noticed / what flew among us unless it was weighted and bound in its mask."

Right. And what does that say to you?

That consciousness is needed again. I think that because I'm white, because I haven't known the underbelly of racism as you have, I see the poem as a strong, sensual tribute to a woman who simply does not realize her own beauty.

Her real beauty.

And I don't feel race in the poem, although I know it's there. Probably because I feel myself a woman before I feel myself white — which is something that apparently is possible because I was born into the ethnic group that holds the bulk of power in this country.

You're really right to follow what we've been talking about with this poem. I believe that consciousness can be sought and found by opening many doors. And I think that what I'm finding more and more in my work is the connections between what is most intimate and what is most vast—the forces we think of as being not familial, not intimate. We try to separate our lives into this social construction and this familial construction, and I am seeing more and more how what I'm always writing about is intimacy, and how when I'm writing about intimacy, I'm always writing about society. The realization that "the personal is political."

And the individual is universal?

Yeah. That's how it was stated earlier, before politics were allowed, when it had to be ivory tower. And there are people with a lot of clout who still want that ivory tower. So here we are again, back at double consciousness and how each of has to straddle the line between what the artist has to do — which as Matisse says is turn himself inside out, and the other questions about communication. How do you reach people? How do you express, how do you find language that contains both this personal deconstruction and unmasking but also what is recognizable as a language that speaks to a community of listeners? That's very difficult for me. Sometimes I have to leave behind some parts of myself, and I've had to accept a kind of internal tension to use constructions that I know will be "acceptable." It seems to me that's part of the tension that may hold my work together.

Isn't that also part of the 'Catch-22' of art? Which is that when you have done all that to find the image, the metaphor, the line that will be at least relatively acceptable, sometimes it isn't.

Sometimes you have to fly in the face of opposition. Again — if we ask is the process different for a black writer and a white writer, I don't know. I'd have to go nuance by nuance trying to separate out some of the distinctions of that journey. But certainly all of these large questions go in the same arena. It's about being an artist. Maybe the most important thing is to think about how we can speak to each other, what is the dialog about this process? How can this become enlivening? Can we acknowledge these nuances and thus enliven our art?

Well, certainly nuance matters, yet when I read "Christmas Eve. . ." that woman could be my mother, I could be that little girl. I could even be the mother. So maybe we need to include the individual/universal aspect . . .

Well, James Baldwin said he didn't write about race because its the only thing he could write about. He wrote about it because it was the door he had to go through to write about other things. That's part of a way, perhaps, of peeling back experience too. Because everything is a metaphor. I don't care what you're writing about — if it's mother/daughter you're using that as a metaphor for speaking of the human experiences that we all have of feeling different or feeling love or loneliness or despair. This is the material we have to make these internal processes visible. But the poem is trying to let us see through these metaphors, to really touch what it is to be human and alive, and that's (in a way) the great comfort of poetry, how we can hopefully read not by taking a black writer and sticking him over here — okay, he's a black writer, now I'm going to read about being black. Not that kind of reading, but to pick it up and look through this, see what it's like to be human, to see how it relates to me, to who I am, to my sameness and otherness. As you say, it's an experience that's universal maybe in the way you relate to your mother, or child, that some experience of self and other translates to very basic experiences.

It's hard to imagine an effective counter-argument to that.

I hope so. I've spent a long time getting to be able to articulate it so that, hopefully, people can *not* get defensive. That's the hard thing for writers — particularly black or minority writers, women — to express complexity so that people can see the larger shaping concept around it.

Have you considered the reverse that can come from the audience? Where a white reader voices frustration at a minority writer "rubbing it in our faces" that he or she is black, or Jewish, or Hispanic . . .

I'm glad you said that. What I think is going on there is that consciousness can be very destructive. For instance, one of my white students said to me *I am so sick of you just rubbing this in our faces. We're reading all these black writers in this class, and you're just rubbing it in our face.* So I said *Well, how many black writers have you read in your life? One? Six maybe? And this is "rubbing it in your face?"* The point is that the mind is very self-protective, and the ego and reality are constructed as a defense, partly, and when new information and new ways one has to shape self and others start emerging, it's scary! It hurts. So that what you do is blame it on the other person "rubbing it in your face." It's sort of making her the powerful one. Of course, one of the stereotypes about black people is that they're physically aggressive. This is part of the whole thing — black people are physical, they're not mental, they can't think very well. *Well here's a writer — black and with a commanding presence — and she's "rubbing it in my face.* So this, from a white perspective, is not only a defense. It's a justification for her then having a very strong defense against allowing anything that woman says to touch her. She is feeling that she's being attacked by this woman's presence. Therefore she's justified in her own defense against opening and learning something about who this woman really is. You have to understand what people are trying to protect.

I wonder if we need to be conscious that when a white teacher stands in front of a classroom, she may be "rubbing in the face" of every minority student a distasteful ethnic presence.

No. I think there's a difference here. I think that the white student might perceive a minority figure as "rubbing it in her face." She has made that figure the violator. I'm not so sure, though, that your black students, for example, are making you the violator in the same way. I just want to say that this is part of the construction of racism in our society. In a way, the person who responds so negatively to a black writer is just relying on a cliche about black people. She's just restating and relying on a cliché that black people are aggressive and violent and want to in some way humiliate you. It may even be a sexual kind of reference.

Possibly, although a more generalized notion of physical aggression seems to be enough.

Well, there was a woman I worked with who had this response to me. She felt that I was overpowering her in her position as a white woman, that I was asking her to do a certain kind of work in her writing. And I said to her *Why don't you start exploring these feelings that I am a powerful person overwhelming you?* She's a very courageous woman who began really exploring that. She began writing about a girl in her childhood, a black girl in the school that she went to, who used to get into fights, and who intimidated her. She was afraid of this little black girl. And she associated me with this girl. Then she began to write about how she came to school. As a result of her family relationships, she was set up to find someone to overpower her. That's how she was treated in her own family. She couldn't speak. She was intimidated by her father, and in a way her whole life had followed this infantile construction about power and finding people to be the powerful ones and she the less powerful. As a result of writing this, not only did that pattern become clear, she also began to see some of the subtle ways in which she had been complicit in this — not only in a personal way, but in a cultural way, in a social way. For example, the only white teacher that had empowered her was a teacher who was not kind to the black children in the school. But because this person empowered her, she never spoke up to this woman about what she observed because she was so glad to find someone who empowered her. So again, that shows how these matters are subtle and complicated. And in the final piece she wrote, she realized that this young girl, and all of the black kids — none of them went to high school. And she had-n't realized the significance of the larger drama unfolding in the lives of these children, that these kids were counseled into jobs, and told *Well, you don't want to go to high school because it'll just be hard for you to be there.* And these people are saying these things as if they're being kind! And that's where we get back to the artists' colony. We would like to think that just because we get educated or we're conscious, we're not going to do things that seem really stupid.

Right.

You know, girls are told *Make sure your boyfriend uses a condom.* As if when we give out that knowledge we're going to stop these powerful hormonal and psychic drives that — it's like the infor-mation we give is a pimple on a whale's behind. There's so much more operating than what we have conscious control over. There again! That tension between consciousness and what's not con-scious. It's very mysterious. But then that's the way life is when we really don't try to make it one thing or another. I don't know what it is. And that's the thing. I just don't know.

Maybe what we find out if we do the hard work of writing is that it's a way of finding out continually . . .

That's it exactly. And for me there's no place of final security or platform to speak from. I'm just part of a process. I'm trying to finish this book, *The Black Notebooks*, and the deadline is less than a month away. And I'm still saying to myself, *If I could just get through with this I'd be done with writing about all this black stuff.* (Laughter) Like, this is going to be my final statement!

When will the book come out?

Next spring, I think.

Well, it will be good to see it in print. All those little boxes, big boxes.

I'm glad I thought about that. It's like making a home for me. I have to think more about it.

There might be another metaphor at work — the way that we get "boxed in" by circumstance.

Oh, yeah!

That's a nice little deconstructive maneuver you've got going on with boxes . . . and to think we started this conversation with Allen Ginsberg, who is now practically an institution.

(Laughter) Right. And not necessarily a "nice" man.

Well, no one is necessarily nice.

To get that together is never easy for me.

Still, to dismiss the work because of the artist's personal short-comings is almost surely an error.

Yes. And in the evolving of one's powers of expression, sometimes one has to do things that — well — ya just gotta do what ya gotta do, so sometimes ya gotta make certain parts of your internal voice — ya just gotta tell it to shut up. Some student said, *Every time I read* Moby Dick, *I can't write for another five years.* So the teacher said, *Okay, don't read* Moby Dick. I guess at certain times, in order to feel empowered, you may have to leave out a part of something that makes you feel you can't express yourself. And that's part of development.

Books

Today Lorca and Pound
fell off my shelf.
They lay there on the floor
like a couple of drunks.
How humble are the lives
of books!
How small their expectations!
They wait quietly,
pressed together
to be called into
the light. When you open them,
they tell you everything
they know. They exhaust
you, like convicts
or madmen
too eager to talk.

Hamtramck: The Polish Women

What happens to the beautiful girls with slender hips and
    bright round dresses?
One day they disappear without leaving a trace of themselves,
and the next they appear again, dragging a heavy
    shopping cart from the bakery to the pork store with
    packages of greasy sausage and potatoes.
Like old nuns they waddle down the main street, past the rich
    gaudy cathedral with the little infant of Prague — in
    real clothes — linens they tend lovingly, starch in
    steamy buckets (their hands thick as potatoes, white),
    and iron with dignity.

The Friendship

I tell you I am angry.
You say you are afraid.
You take your glasses off and lay
them on the table like a sparkling weapon.
I hold my purse in front of me.
Do I love you? Do you love me?
"If we just had time . . ."

You could show me how you wore your hair
pushed forward over one eye, hiding
half of what you knew of beauty.

Poor friendship, why must it sit
at a table where the waitress
is ready to go home? In a city
between tunnels — cracks
of darkness in the sea.

Allen Ginsberg

Once Allen Ginsberg stopped to pee at a bookstore
  in New Jersey,
but he looked like a bum —
    not like the miracle laden Christ with electric atom juice,
    not like the one whose brain is a river in which was plunked
    the stone of the world (the one bathing fluid to wash away
    25,000 year half-lives), he was dressed as a bum.
He had wobbled on a pee-heavy bladder
in search of a gas station,
a dime store with a quarter booth,
a Chinese restaurant,
when he came to that grocery store of dreams:
Chunks of Beaudelaire's skin
glittered in plastic;
his eyes in sets, innocent
as the unhoused eyes of a butchered cow.
In a dark corner, Rimbaud's
genitals hung like jerky,
and the milk of Whitman's breasts
drifted in a carton, dry as talcum.
He wanted to pee and lay his head
on the cool stacks;
but the clerk took one look
and thought of the buttocks of clean businessmen squatting
  during their lunch hour,
the thin flanks of pretty girls buying poetry for school.
Behind her, faintly, the deodorized bathroom.
She was the one at the gate

protecting civilization.
He turned, walked to the gutter,
unzipped his pants, and peed.
Do you know who that was?
A man in the back came forth.
Soon she was known as
The woman in the story on Main
who said no to Allen Ginsberg;
and she is proud—
so proud she told this story
pointing to the spot outside, as if
still flowed that holy stream.

On the Turning Up
of Unidentified Black Female Corpses

Mowing his three acres with a tractor,
a man notices something ahead — a mannequin —
he thinks someone threw it from a car. Closer
he sees it is the body of a black woman.

The medics come and turn her with pitchforks.
Her gaze shoots past him to nothing. Nothing
is explained. How many black women
have been turned up to stare at us blankly,

in weedy fields, off highways,
pushed out in plastic bags,
shot, knifed, unclothed partially, raped,
their wounds sealed with a powdery crust.

Last week on TV, a gruesome face, eyes bloated shut.
No one will say, "She looks like she's sleeping," ropes
of blue-black slashes at the mouth. Does anybody
know this woman? Will anyone come forth? Silence

like a backwave rushes into that field
where, just the week before, four other black girls
had been found. The gritty image hangs in the air
just a few seconds, but it strikes me,

a black woman, there is a question being asked
about my life. How can I
protect myself? Even if I lock my doors,
walk only in the light, someone wants me dead.

Am I wrong to think
if five white women had been stripped,
broken, the sirens would wail until
someone was named?

Is it any wonder I walk over these bodies
pretending they are not mine, that I do not know
the killer, that I am just like any woman —
if not wanted, at least tolerated.

Part of me wants to disappear, to pull
the earth on top of me. Then there is this part
that digs me up with this pen
and turns my sad black face to the light.

A Note on My Son's Face

I.

Tonight, I look, thunderstruck
at the gold head of my grandchild.
Almost asleep, he buries his feet
between my thighs;
his little straw eyes
close in the near dark.
I smell the warmth of his raw
slightly foul breath, the new death
waiting to rot inside him.
Our breaths equalize our heartbeats;
every muscle of the chest uncoils,
the arm bones loosen in the nest
of nerves. I think of the peace
of walking through the house,
pointing to the name of this, the name of that,
an educator of a new man.

Mother. Grandmother. Wise
Snake-woman who will show the way;
Spider-woman whose tentacles
hold him precious. Or will tear off his head,
her teeth over the little husband,
the small fist clotted in trust at her breast.

This morning, looking at the face of his father,
I remembered how, an infant, his face was too dark,
nose too broad, mouth too wide.
I did not look in the mirror
and see the face that could save me
from my own darkness.
Did he, looking in my eye, see
what I turned from:
my own dark grandmother
bending over gladioli in the field,
her shaking black hand defenseless
at the shining cock of flower?

I wanted that face to die,
to be reborn in the face of a white child.
I wanted the soul to stay the same,
but I loved to death,
to damnation and God-death,
the soul that broke out of me.
I crowed: My son! My Beautiful!
But when I peeked in the basket,
I saw the face of a black man.

Did I bend over his nose
and straighten it with my fingers
like a vine growing the wrong way?
Did he feel my hand in malice?

Generations we fucked
and prayed for this light child,
a shining God of the second coming.

We bow down in shame
and carry the children of the past
in our wallets, begging for forgiveness.

II.

A picture in a book,
a lynching.
The bland faces of men who watch
a Christ go up in flames, smiling,
as if he were a hooked
fish, a felled antelope, some
wild thing tied to boards and burned.
His charring body
gives off light — a halo
burns out of him.
His face scorched featureless;
the hair matted to the scalp
like feathers.
One man stands with his hand on his hip,
another with his arm
slung over the shoulder of a friend,
as if this moment were large enough
to hold affection.

III.

How can we wake
from a dream
we are born into,
that shines around us,
the terrible bright air?

Having awakened,
having seen our own bloody hands,
how can we ask forgiveness,
bring before our children the real
monster of their nightmares?

The worst is true.
Everything you did not want to know.

Christmas Eve: My Mother Dressing

My mother was not impressed with her beauty;
once a year she put it on like a costume,
plaited her black hair, slick as cornsilk, down past her hips,
in one rope-thick braid, turned it, carefully, hand over hand,
and fixed it at the nape of her neck, stiff and elegant as a crown,
with tortoise pins, like huge insects,
some belonging to her dead mother,
some to my living grandmother.
Sitting on the stool at the mirror,
she applied a peachy foundation that seemed to hold her down, to
   trap her;
as if we never would have noticed what flew among us unless it was
   weighted and bound in its mask.
Vaseline shined her eyebrows,
mascara blackened her lashes until they swept down like feathers,
darkening our thoughts of her.
Her eyes deepened until they shone from far away.

Now I remember her hands, her poor hands, which even then were
   old from scrubbing,
whiter on the inside than they should have been,
and hard, the first joints of her fingers, little fattened pads,
the nails filed to sharp points like old-fashioned in pens, painted a
   jolly color:
Her hands stood next to her face and wanted to be put away,
   prayed
for the scrub bucket and brush to make them useful.
And as I write, I forget the years I watched
her pull hairs like a witch from her chin, magnify
every blotch— as if acid were thrown from the inside.

But once a year my mother
rose in her white silk slip,
not the slave of the house, the woman,
took the ironed dress from the hanger —
allowing me to stand on the bed, so that
my face looked directly into her face,
and hold the garment away from her
as she pulled it down.

Linda Hogan

Some Change in the World

*L*inda Hogan's career in writing spans a quarter century *of work that is, by any standard imaginable, impressive for its quality as well as for its variety of genre. Her first book of poems* Calling Myself Home *(Greenfield Review Press, 1979) was followed in two years by another collection of poems,* Daughters, I Love You *(Loretto Heights Women's Research Center, 1981) and the production of a three-act play,* A Piece of the Moon, *produced at the University of Oklahoma in Stillwater. Other books of poems are* Eclipse *(American Indian Studies Center, UCLA, 1983),* Seeing Through the Sun *(University of Massachusetts Press,*

1985), *Savings: Poems* (Coffee House Press, 1988), and *Book of Medicines* (Coffee House Press, 1993). Her books of fiction include two volumes of short stories, *That Horse* (Pueblo of Acoma Press, 1985) and the novels, *Mean Spirit: A Novel* (Atheneum, 1990), *Solar Storms* (Simon and Schuster, 1995) and *Power* (1998). She is also the author of two screenplays, *Mean Spirit* (1996) and *Aunt Moon* (1996), and a book of essays *Dwellings: a Spiritual History of the Living World* (Norton, 1995). She has contributed to *What Moves Me Brings Me to Myself,* edited by Lynda Koolish (Indiana U. Press,) and *I Tell You Now* (University of Nebraska Press, 1987) and edited (with Carol Buechal and Judith McDaniel) *The Stories We Hold Secret: Tales of Women's Spiritual Development* (Greenfield Review Press, 1986). With Brenda Peterson and Deena Metzger, she co-edited *Intimate Nature: The Bond Between Women and Animals* (Ballantine, 1998).

Hogan has received significant public recognition for her writing, including the Five Civilized Tribes Playwriting Award (for *A Piece of the Moon*), a National Endowment for the Arts Fellowship, a Guggenheim, and Lannan Foundation Award. *Mean Spirit* was a finalist for a Pulitzer and *Book of Medicines*, Hogan's most recent book of poems, was a finalist in the National Book Critics Circle Award. Although, on one level, Hogan draws on her tribal identification and the experience of Native American Peoples, she perceives her work as an ongoing part of the life of a global community. She is actively involved in working for wildlife rehabilitation, and seeks to better understand the relationship of species to species, species to world, believing that this is necessary if humanity is to develop necessary survival skills for the future.

Hogan was born Linda Henderson, on July 16, 1947, to Charles and Cleona (Bower) Henderson. Because her father was in the armed services, the Hendersons travelled during her childhood, frequently returning to Oklahoma where her father's family lived on allotment land. Today, Hogan speaks with great fondness of her childhood time in Oklahoma with her Chickasaw grandparents and other family members, describing the warmth and emotional comfort of that environment. During her marriage to Patrick Hogan, the couple adopted two daughters, Sandra Dawn Protector and Tanya Thunder Horse.

Subsequent to high school graduation, Hogan worked at a number of jobs, including dental assistant, teacher's aide, secretary, waitress and nurse's aide. Although college did not originally seem to be a possible pursuit for a young mixed-blood woman without much of an income, Hogan did pursue both undergraduate and graduate degrees, completing her MA at the University of Colorado at Boulder in 1978. Since that time her employment has consisted primarily of teaching posts. She has served as a Poet in the Schools in both Colorado and Oklahoma, and has taught at the University of Colorado-Boulder, Arvada Center for the Performing Arts, and Colorado Women's College.

Although she has travelled in areas as diverse as Germany, France, Mexico and Japan, Hogan is self-described as comfortably rooted in her house. She balances the demands of her writing life and her teaching post with family and friends. Like many, Hogan lives the disciplined life of a writer upon whom too many demands are placed, in her case a life also complicated by chronic illness. Always drawn to nature, she finds "relief" in walking, drawing, and gardening, although she is also an avid, wide-ranging reader.

Although you were born in Denver, you grew up in Oklahoma. . .

My family is *from* Oklahoma, and my Dad was in the army, so we travelled the country. Most of my family remained in Oklahoma and are still there. I consider myself to be a double citizen of Colorado and Oklahoma. My family's from the area that's close to Ardmore. Gene Autry, Oklahoma is the name of the place. The land is allotment land, not reservation. Then my father came here— his older brother Wesley came here to Denver. This was during the fifties, during the relocation, and he formed, with others, the association called the White Buffalo Council, which is still in existence. In fact, a couple of days ago I visited with another founder of the council. My father, too, was back and forth between Oklahoma and Colorado and had by then been in the military and gone to World War II. Later, he was stationed in Colorado Springs. He had a medical discharge when I was about fifteen, after we lived in Germany. Now, I've lived in the same house here for about nineteen years. Even when I took a job in Minnesota, I kept this house. I love it here. Most of my family is still in Oklahoma, so we go back. My parents live in Colorado Springs, and we go back to Oklahoma from time to time. My Dad and I made a trip once some years ago to interview elders.

It must be a little like having your feet in two worlds — or at least two parts of a complicated planet. So you were fifteen when you father was discharged?

Yes. That's when we moved to Colorado Springs.

As a youngster, did you find the contrast between Colorado and Oklahoma unsettling?

If you mean culturally, there's a very strong Indian community here that my family was part of. What changed was that we were in, really not a city, but we certainly weren't in a rural area. In Oklahoma my family lived in rural areas. In fact, the picture on *Calling Myself Home* is a picture of my sister and me and my grandfather going into the town [Gene Autry] to get water. There was no water where my grandparents lived. There was a community pump in town and we went on horses and wagons. So the changes were those contrasts between town and rural life. I have to say that to this day I prefer the rural. (Laughter)

Why is that?

Because there was always love there, and it was an extended family, so that my cousins were always there and my aunts and uncles. I was well cared for by my people, you know, and my grandmother was a very strong, beautiful, *kind* woman that we all worshiped and still do. In Colorado it was a very cold sort of isolated, lonely, individualistic kind of life and culture. Also, I am nurtured by the environment and I care for the land and animals that are not easy to find in towns and cities.

In a way, this relates to a question about the meaning of home. Has the meaning of that word shifted for you over the years since you gave your first book the title Calling Myself Home?

First books, for many people, seem to be sort of autobiographical incursions into who they are, and what it means to be who they are. I think that my first book(of course it was written such a long time ago) but in it the idea of home and identity were the main questions that asked the book into existence. Now of course, partly because I'm older, more mature and hopefully a little more intelligent, I really think of home in a more global context. I feel very rooted in my house here, but to think of home in terms of one small place with one group of people living on it, while it might be the world to that group of people, there are still all the things that are going on in a larger picture that need to be taken into consideration. The planet is so much smaller than we ever thought in the past. I think of the whole planet as home, a whole ecosystem that seems important to our growth as people and our survival.

You referred to Calling Myself Home. *There's a poem in that first book called "Song for my Name." Do you remember that one in any particular way?*

It's one that young people always love.

It's very insistent in its preoccupation with all of the history, the inherited things, that create a name, and also with where names go, which you say in the poem is "back to the earth." What were the circumstances of writing that poem?

Well, as I said, that entire book really is a kind of question of belonging — who are the people you belong with, where is the place, what is the individual in that world?

I noticed that the notes on the author in Calling Myself Home *identify you as "Chickasaw and white." I was intrigued that in the more recent books you're described as Chickasaw or Native American, but not as mixed blood. Was that an intentional thing?*

No. I don't think so. I think it just happened that way. Although

I have to say that for Indian people — and I don't know if it's memory, genetics, or culture, but an understanding of the world through native eyes is stronger than for the non-Indian part of a person who is of mixed blood. Most of my friends who are mixed blood don't claim any white heritage. They just go ahead and identify as the tribe with which they are affiliated. I often feel like it's important to acknowledge both sides. Particularly for the younger writers, some of the conflicts that are in the work come from being of mixed heritage. Myself, I am happier and more at home in the Indian community, enough so that sometimes I think about disappearing from the dominating world permanently.

Well, that's certainly an option.

Yes. I can do that. I think about it. I'm probably a little young to do it. I feel like some of the work I've been doing this last year is important to share with people of European background. And there are characters in my work who do take that direction.

Now you've reminded me of a poem in Seeing through the Sun *that starts out "In my left pocket, a Chickasaw hand/. . . In my right pocket / a white hand. Don't worry, it's mine, / not some thief's." That's one tension. Then further down the page, you give your reader coins and keys that have "the sharp teeth of property." Could you elaborate on that?*

Well, of course property is an abstract economic concept based on a hidden dollar that has been the cause of the death of people. Business interests internationally stand to gain even now by losing native people, indigenous people. I was just at a United Nations meeting about two weeks ago, and that was the focus of the group — human rights in the presence of governments and corporations that want monetary gain from the land and the people. In fact, pharmaceutical companies from the United States have gone into the Amazon area and discovered tribes that nobody knew were there until they started building highways and logging roads. They have forced people to sign agreements saying that they would give over medicinal plants and knowledge about those plants to pharmaceutical companies. I mean this country and most others that work out of our economic system are founded on the idea of property, and most of the transgressions that take place here have to do with property. There were massive slaughters of some of the California tribes during the gold rush, and the same thing happened to the Cherokee in Georgia. So, you know, property is no insignificant thing for us to think about if we ever want to change the world.

I can't help wondering if it's property, specifically, or the power that property represents.

It's both of those. The legal power, the monetary power, the control issues. For instance, look at the telescope project on Mt. Graham. That's not even the best place to build the particular type of telescope that they're talking about, but it has become an issue of control, and so the fight continues because — for no good reason really — those with power don't want to set a precedent, cannot permit the people, whose sacred ground is Mt. Graham, to appear to win a legal struggle.

The childishness of that attitude — that insistence on "mine" and "my way only" — is rather frightening.

Right. Torture and genocide are based on such small words as those.

And still, almost surprisingly, as a species, we produce art. When did you start writing? How old were you?

I was in my late twenties.

And where were you, at that point?

I was married and living in Maryland, where my husband was going to school, and I was working as a teacher's aide. When I discovered writing, it was like finding — like being dropped into water and finding that you're an excellent swimmer — that you love the water and you love to swim. I think when I discovered poetry it allowed me to step into my real life, my real self — the body, heart and soul of being alive.

One thing interesting about that is the age you were. So many women begin writing what I would call "late." I started at forty, Susan Ludvigson when she was married and a mother with a teaching career, you in your late twenties. . .Why do you suppose that more women don't come to writing earlier than they do? Yourself, for example. You had "arrived" in a sense. You were married, had left your childhood home, were embarked on the "finished" stage of being a married woman.

Well, I don't think we — and I'm speaking for myself, largely — think about it as a possibility for ourselves. I don't think we know how magical and transforming it is. Or maybe we think we don't have much to say.

Or that someone else has already said it, perhaps, and we're superfluous?

And that's almost always the case. Not the superfluous part. One of my friends says that no matter where she goes, she find some poet's already been in that territory. (Laughter)

(Laughter) Or a novelist, or an essayist, or even a stand-up comic. Do you count any specific mentors or influences in your early years as a writer?

There really were not. My family — my Dad and my uncles and my grandmother my other family members — were wonderful storytellers. At one point I began to realize that what they were saying was important and that nobody was writing it down, or preserving it. I'm sure that there were always people remembering the stories, but my thought at the time was that perhaps there weren't. So I went through a period of writing down, first, *Calling Myself Home*, about growing up in Oklahoma and about my childhood and the little secrets of our home, and then about living in the projects in Colorado Springs. I wrote short stories about that. Now I look at it in a larger way and I think place has been a mentor for me, and nature. I have always mostly been interested in this world around us, and that's not always the human world. I believe these things have been directions for me more than individual people have been. They have been maps to my growing mind, religions to my heart.

Do you feel connections between specific places and specific kinds of language?

Yes. Language is really connected to place. In native languages, indigenous languages, for example. One of the things people don't think about very often is that English is a very *small* language. It has only a tenth, sometimes less, of the vocabulary of some of the native languages and for indigenous people who come from a place, an ecosystem — the relationship to that place is actually embedded in the language itself. Individual words refer to entire systems and one word will open out into a variety of meanings that take in and summon together an entire region of the world. And in Navajo, a friend tells me, there are over 36,000 words for motion, alone.

So that's an organic quality that, say, a colonial language wouldn't have.

Right. And it shapes the thinking and perception, even the sciences and mappings, of people who have that language. You can see how that, in turn, can call for a history and mythic world and science that is different than in English.

Of course. But the users of language also shape it. I wonder how that works in terms of writing. When you were working on Solar Storms, for instance, how many years of conscious work — which might be you shaping the language in particular ways — went into that novel?

I have no idea! I really don't. I don't know if you mean conscious work where I'm sitting focused on the novel, or the development of a conscious mind. The book is about certain events that are historical, contemporary events. It's a fictionalized story of the Hydro-Quebec James Bay project. And this kind of exploitation of land and people has always been on my mind. I suppose it takes a lifetime of reflection and thought to move a writer in a certain direction. But the time I needed to write this book was maybe three or four years.

Solar Storms is such an astonishingly powerful and moving book that it took me several readings to be able to think critically about it. The Book of Medicines affected me the same way. As you were working on those, were you conscious that the books were in any way different from the books that had preceded them?

Different in the way they're written? Different in what they're about?

Different in the way you thought about them when you were writing them. Solar Storms *and* The Book of Medicines *both are ripe, mature — meticulously crafted with a vision and level of skill that weren't quite as evident in the earlier books, good as they are. There are no chinks in these two, no false moves that I can find.*

Well, I had written more fiction, so I had some experience behind me when I wrote *Solar Storms.* I am very careful with how things are put down, with their order. I revise a great deal. That's one of my secrets, a lot of revision. I've trained myself, really, as a poet. So I care about the words and how they sound, look, and feel. And I think the poetry is a basic language for writing, the most condensed, every word cared about. It's preparation for all the other shapes and kinds of writing.

I think that's very evident in Solar Storms.

I don't feel like only narrative can carry a story. For me it needs to be put together in a way that is the best the language can do. I care about it being beautiful. I suppose another part of it is that I'm older, and I'm still learning about life, although I admit that every time I start a new project, it's like I've never learned anything. But still there is a bit of a foundation and I feel like the book is about not only one place and one event that happened — or the two events — the girl Angela going home to find her birth family and the protest at the dam building. But I feel like these stories are really larger stories about what has happened in the world and what shouldn't have happened.

The same story is being played out daily in one part of the

world or another. "Story" is significant here, the stories we tell ourselves, those we learn. So I think stories contribute to what we will continue to allow to happen in and out of our world. I've observed that when people do political work, they might go and talk to people about *You need to speak out about this*, or *You need do that*, and everyone gets excited and they're ready to do it. Then a day or two later they go back to their lives and business goes on as usual. But when there's an emotional element, a story, with characters you grow to care about, then I think it actually makes a difference in the world, and that's why I write. Because story has a power. Because I've seen it make a difference, seen it change people. In the last years, I've been involved in the native science dialogues. These gatherings bring together indigenous knowledge with the intellectual systems of western-based knowledge. This dialogue/education has had a significant effect on me, my work. Now my work takes in more of the differences and confluences between cultures and puts them together a little more clearly in stories, essays, poems.

There's a quality of myth, too, or at least a strong mythic level in both Solar Storms *and* The Book of Medicines *that is extremely potent — I don't know another word to describe it — that seems to be related to these possibilities of dialog between two elements. In a talk with Wendy Rose that you taped for the Lannan Foundation you suggested that one reason you like amphibians is that they represent an ability to live in two elements. . .*

(Laughter) Well, you know I love all animals and nature. I just find that the more I learn about the world the more exciting and fascinating it all is. The other day we went to what's called a medicine garden. High school students in this area have put together a circular garden of traditional plants, and the corn in this garden, the kernels it grew from, is at least 200 years old, probably older. Nobody knows exactly. But it's a native corn that hasn't been grown in over 200 years. Native American students at the Eagle Lodge in Denver had planted some of the kernels. We were all standing around the garden, and I looked down and saw this spider that had built its little hole in the earth where its home is, and it had taken some of the straw that was on the ground in the garden, and woven it into a perfect design around that hole. It was really beautiful. To me, the fact that the spider did that, a design woven of straw, is really pretty amazing. It knows how to create its home and how to do art. And the more I observe the world, the more I learn about it, the more I think that there's a vast terrestrial intelligence all around us.

You've just reminded me of the closing poem in The Book of Medicines, *"The Origin of Corn." One of the most compelling things about that poem, despite the depth of pain, or maybe sorrow, that is contained in the book, is the way it knits things back together on a note of hope that plants will still find this world "green and alive." How do you sustain that hopeful vision in a world that appears, in many ways, to have gone insane?*

I don't know, but I always have faith. I think that things may yet be all right. And for all of the damage, the world still is pretty resilient. I do find that these are very difficult times. I don't hold to total optimism. It's just a balance so that a person doesn't fall into despair that renders them helpless, joyless, apathetic. I know that we're even emptying the oceans — there's such widespread damage.

Well, there's certainly no shortage of that. And you've observed tremendous changes since you were a youngster who was close to nature, but who owed that, maybe, to the fact that she grew from rural poverty.

Yes. And I hadn't even thought of going to school. It was out of my reach, and didn't even occur to me. When my father was in the military he was an enlisted man, and the class structure is deeply a part of the military. Then when I went to California, I met my cousin Sakej Henderson. My cousin was a college student. And he had very interesting friends and they had interesting lives compared to mine. They didn't have to work all the time for one thing. (Laughter) It was because of my cousin that I later decided to go to school. And actually, the thing that is very interesting is that I feel we're really close now. He lives in Canada. His wife is a Micmac and she says *What is it with you Chickasaws? You're always trying to save the world!* And he is, too. He works with the United Nations. He's very hardworking for indigenous human rights. That was what got me to school. It was meeting these people who went to school. I never even knew what a professor was, and now I am one, although somewhat reluctantly even now. (Laughter)

What was it that pulled you into the professoriate, finally?

I fell into it. It wasn't something that I picked. If I'd had a choice and made the decision when I was younger about what I wanted to do, I would've been a veterinarian. I never wanted to be a writer, either, but I suppose we each find a calling and fall into it.

Didn't your first book came out about two years after you began teaching on the college level?

Well, I was teaching while I was still in graduate school, and I wrote the book *Calling Myself Home* while I was a student.

Was there a connection, then, between school and the writing, or the publication of the writing?

No. I've been very fortunate with my writing work compared to some other people. I know people who send books off and they don't get accepted. My first book came into being with Joe Bruchac at the Greenfield Review Press. He was involved with a literary magazine at the time, and he saw my work and asked me if I had enough to make a book. So I went through and looked and put together a collection of poems and that became *Calling Myself Home*. That was a difficult time in some ways, because it changed my life so much. The writing has, that is. The book was taken up in classrooms. It was being taught. There were not a lot of contemporary mixed blood people writing at the time, so it seemed to open up a way for people to begin thinking about the experience, for other writers to begin talking about it. And I was being invited to go talk about the book and give readings. That was back in 1978. I had no idea. I was immature and I had to work very hard to educate myself to be able to talk about it. It's been quite a life, I have to say. I've been carried along with it. A wonderful life.

Do you remember your first reading with any specificity?

My first public reading? I do. I didn't want to do it. It's frightening, when you don't know what you're doing, to stand up and read. Now I'm used to it and it doesn't bother me, but it was pretty difficult. I had a teacher who was a bit of an alcoholic, like so many people in those days. He recommended a little rum before your readings. And I did that, which was very stupid of me. I mean, I got through the reading pretty well without appearing to be drunk, but it was bad advice. I especially see that when I see how many drinking writers there are in the world, and I worry about them, because I don't think that they can keep up the writing life and be drinkers too.

I don't think one can either. Like you, I know writers that I'm concerned about because I'm afraid they are unknowing alcoholics. It's as if they're absent from life, in some way. I find that frightening.

You know, Richard Hugo talks about that in "The Triggering Town." Also, writers, he says, get very caught up in the idea that their work and they are the same thing, instead of thinking of the work as something apart from them. So if they do well as writers, it causes inner conflict because of self-esteem. I see that with students a lot, where any conversation about their work is taken very personally. I think they have to learn to be professional listeners — you know — see if they can use the information, make some of the changes, whatever. . .

That's especially hard for young writers, I suppose. But then a lot is hard for young writers, including the balance of work and personal life. Did you find that when you were an "emerging" writer? How did the stress of marriage, childrearing, divorce. . . all work with your writing life?

We got divorced shortly after we adopted the girls, so I've been single since 1981.

That's a long time, and a lot of responsibility while your daughters were younger. The official change in marital status is a significant marker in life. If you could do it over, what would you change?

In my marriage or in my life?

Either. Both.

I don't know that I would really make any changes. Everything has worked out very well, even though a person never feels at the time that it will be okay. I wouldn't have chosen a different family, or different background at all. I don't think I would make any changes. I actually like my life.

That's such a good thing! — to like one's life.

I know. They say it's a sign of health when you prefer your own crazy family over everyone else's crazy family. (Laughter)

I think that's probably true.

You know, I think the one thing that I would change — still that I would like to change — is that I'm very shy. I would really love to talk more with other people but I don't often do it because I feel intimidated easily. I think that's very much a human quality, but I'm very much an introvert, and sometimes I think it'd be nice to be very extroverted. But it's not in my nature.

(Laughter) To me, that's both wonderful and ironic. Before we began talking, you seemed to me to have a dignity and reserve that I found a little unnerving, and a little awe-inspiring, and I would never have guessed that you were shy.

You know, whatever it is that speaks through me does a really good job. (Laughter)

I would say! Is shyness a problem for you in the classroom? Do you find yourself uncomfortable in that smaller setting?

What bothers me more in the classroom than discomfort over being shy is that I am not an intellectual, and my students usually value the intellectual life over writing. I have a very hard time with that. I feel like my job isn't teaching the environmental essay or fiction or poetry; it's teaching students to become writers, to think of themselves as writers, to think of writing as valid work. Since most of the students really think or believe that they will grow up to become professors who write on the side, they begin to learn things that are against their work — that go against the writing, the creative life. But they don't ever believe that and I watch many a promising writer give up the work — the creative work — for a PhD program.

Well, in a sense they're children — at least as writers — so how much can they be expected to know of what the creative life entails?

But they think they want to be writers and then this other thing takes over, and that's one of the problems in the western educational system. I have questions and doubts about the validity of that order and that world.

Well, it does seem to me that students who long to be writers, in particular who want to write what we call "creatively" rather than what I sometimes think of as "footnotedly," need an antidote to some of the intellectually conventional ways of looking at writing — and you may be it. You may be the necessary balance within their education. Otherwise, how would they begin to discover possibilities outside the academy?

And I don't know that they do. I'm not sure of that. I mean every once in a while a writer breaks through all that. I was talking with Barbara Kingsolver, and she told me she couldn't even get accepted into a writing program and they wouldn't let her sit in on classes. And yet, you know, she's a best selling writer.

Well yeah! She's a wonderful writer. It astounds me that she couldn't get into a writing program.

There's a kind of snobbery about all this.

There is. I guess if you're on the inside you call it networking, and if you're not you call it cronyism or favoritism or something. But you're right. And people tend to foster and cling to their own asso-

ciations, which may point to a lack of real groundedness on the
part of the system.

Also the commitment about why a person writes. There are won-
derful things to be done with writing — stories are so significant
in everybody's life. But these are too often given up for theory and
other kinds of things that seem important but are really just intel-
lectual exercises.

*(Laughter.) Yes. But think back. When you began writing and pub-
lishing poetry, what do you think made you a poet first, before
you turned to fiction or the essay?*

I loved poetry. I still do. I love the process of writing it, the very
sort of quiet way of being in the world. I think it's more about
being than it is about thinking, and I like that. The only draw-
back was that there were stories I wanted to tell that couldn't be
told in the form of a poem. So I had to figure out how to do
some of those other things, to write in fiction and essays the
stories that I wanted to tell.

When you're writing, do you think much about genre divisions?

No. I'm just writing. I don't really think about genre.

*So you don't sit down and say something like "Today I'm a novel-
ist. Next week or the week after I'll be an essayist, or maybe a
poet."*

Well, actually, no. Right now I'm working on a novel, but I'm also
working on some poems. And I'll sit down . . . I do divide my
time in the day, so that I take the time and I say *Well, okay. Now
it's time to work on this chapter*, and I'll sit down and work on that.
But sometimes, early — I like to write early in the morning — I
get up and I'll start writing poetry or whatever runs through the
mind and hand. It's kind of a clearing time. Although the thing
that's very difficult for writers, once they've been doing it for a
while, is that the demands are very great in other areas. The more
recognition you receive, the less time there is to write unless you
are able to be assertive about your time. You know. Not answer

all the letters, not answer the telephone. I tell my friends when they come over to my house and its cluttered, I'll say *You know, I had a choice. I could work on the book or I could clean my house. So I'm not cleaning the house.* (Laughter) Wouldn't we rather see a person's poems than see their vacuumed floor?

(Laughter) I know. My own tendency is to say "Well, it's the kitchen cabinets or the manuscript. I think I'll just go out." And then I don't do either of the initial tasks, which may not be the best choice.

It depends on what you want to do. If you *really* prefer to go out and do something then that's your choice. That's what you need to do that day. I try to make sure that I get out enough to keep in contact with the rest of the world. (Laughter) So I work, and then I go in the evening or afternoon — not every day — but I usually go visit my family. They're only twenty minutes away. And we get together. Or I go with friends to a movie or supper. But there is definitely not enough time to write. There is never enough time. This keeps me from believing in relativity.

If you did have all the time in the world. . .

I would write. I would write and I'd be outdoors most of the time. I'd have time for horses, poems, stories.

And would you ever be tired at the end of every day!

Yes, but what a wonderful kind of tired.

What do you see as poetry's place in the America today?

One of the reasons I went into other kinds of writing is because I think poetry doesn't have a very strong place in America today, and unless you are in a university setting, you are not likely to read poetry. I know there are people who do it anyway, so I don't mean this as a total generalization. I know that when I'm at work at the university the people there value what other people who work there think of their work. But writing and talking to ordinary people that live in this world — I feel like that's important to do. It's not best for a writer to write just for the people they work with, or who teach English, and yet [the failure] to do so invites a barrage of criticism. The real place of writing is to make change in the world, and it's a very powerful medium. Poetry is the *most* powerful, but it takes training for most people to read poetry, and I think that puts it out of the hands of everyday people.

I can't decide whether I fully agree with that.

Well, I think poetry in other countries is a more powerful medium, and is considered as work. As real work. Employment. It is read. It is loved. It is respected. That seldom happens here.

And at the same time, it appears to be a more vital part of the culture generally. This is a bit of a shift, but I've been wondering about this. When you wrote "Crossings," the poem in which a fetal whale has "the shadow of a human face," and when you wrote in Solar Storms *about Agnes Iron in her bearskin coat being one with the bear, to the extent of seeing the cubs that had grown in that body, how metaphorical were you being? How literal?*

I suppose half and half. Although I don't usually think of metaphor. "Crossings" is about the place where species cross over. Humans were water animals and whales were once land animals, land mammals. I always find it fascinating that we ended up on land and they ended up in water. And that we probably are equally intelligent — maybe they are more intelligent than we are, given the things I learn about them. Their brains have sixty million years more evolution than ours. The poem places, or tries to trace, the point where two species cross into each other's worlds of knowledge.

Two elements again. What about the idea that each of us carries, inside, the knowledge of those other species with whom we share ancestors?

I don't know. If we did we would behave very differently in the world, if we carried that inside ourselves, if we knew other species. And maybe there's the *bodily* knowledge in blood and bone, but it hasn't gotten to our minds as yet, very well. As a species, we haven't yet learned how to treat the rest of the world, how to see, how to know. Daily, in science, the world changes. It's only now coming back to uncover the incredible amount of intelligence that surrounds us in the world, that has, since that European presence here, been completely diminished, seen as not valid, not real, not alive. And now, of course, James Lovelock has come up with the Gaia hypothesis, about the world being alive and related. European-minded people are understanding what tribal people have always said about elephants, that they talk to each other over hundreds of miles in ways and sounds that humans can't hear. Researchers have found, for instance, that planting a garden a certain way makes that garden survive and be effective, but if you plant it another way it doesn't work. In our time, we've been planting our world garden the wrong way and living the wrong way. Our educations have been completely negligent in that respect. Students don't learn in school about the natural world or about the incredible achievements of other species. I sometimes think that when we imagine we know something, that it's mostly conjecture, and that it actually diminishes the world and the animals around us when we imagine that we know what they're about. A more open mind is called for. We're very limited. We have very limited minds. Our equipment for understanding the world is not very evolved. Basically, all we have is our minds.

Yet it seems that there's a kind of suggestion in the presence of shared genetic material that there may be a level of knowledge, cellular perhaps, that we simply are not equipped to tap into. Or if we do, we need to deny it, as if the knowledge might turn us into something like Hannah Wing, who carried so much knowledge of destruction and pain that she became a destroyer.

Yes. She had been tortured, and that was what created her. But I agree. It seems that more and more we are learning about, talking about a knowledge that resides in cell, in DNA, in the basic components of life and matter. It's been in the western history of science that the abstract has been idealized over matter. Until recently. As spirit has been preferred over body in the religious systems.

I'm wondering whether, if we could in some way find that cellular knowledge, we would find some 'final' knowledge of ourselves as the torturers, which could be destructive for the existing identity . . .

Yes, it would be a positive thing if people acknowledged their inner shadows. And would we be identified, I wonder, with the other side of that, as victim, and then would we have another facet, for healer?

And survive it. I suspect that takes not just a particular strength, but preparation . . .

And then to be able to transform it.

Right. When you started The Book of Medicines *with "The History of Red," what made you settle on that specific poem?*

I don't think about these things consciously. I just have a feel for them. And it just felt like it should be there. Also, it establishes and covers all the material in the book. Not as an outline, but more of a clue to the rest of the poems and their direction. It's really a sort of history of human beings coming into learning or knowledge. That includes medicine and the other sciences, creation stories, the world experienced. I do a lot of revision, but I work from something besides my mind, so that when putting poems in place, I am working by feel.

Writing in English, do you ever consider yourself as a producer of multicultural texts?

I don't really think about categories at all, but I suppose that if a native person writes, the material becomes multicultural.

I know that you suffer from a chronic illness. Is that something you're willing to talk about?

I have a couple of things going on. I have a secondary condition called fibro-myalgia. Basically it's an immune system disorder and involves chronic pain. It's an illness that is becoming so prevalent now, a sign of our environmental times. Like Susan Griffin writes about in her work as being a sense of the world dying inside our bodies.

How does that affect your work life?

Some days I am unable to work at anything. I have to stay in bed. After I teach a class, it takes me nearly two days to restore my energy level. But I do better than most of the people with this illness. Doctors even sometimes ask me how I manage so well. I'm very fortunate. When I was first sick I was very sick. I had trouble even dressing myself. But right now I walk about four miles a day on good days to make up for those immobile ones when I can barely walk to another room. And I manage to keep up with my writing and my family. It requires, however, constant body consciousness to know what I can or can't do in any given moment. If I'm not careful, if I do too much, I can lose half a week out of my life.

So you've focused on what is most important in your life?

Yes. I'm on medication, including herbs and homeopathics. I've responded very well to it. Not everybody does that. I know other people who have this. Large numbers of Indians are affected. It's a bit like chronic fatigue or Epstein Barr, although most like the Gulf War Syndrome. These are all in the same category. I think I may have it to a lesser degree than some or I responded to the medication. In native communities this is almost an epidemic. In fact, I've been trying to get a grant to go and interview people, particularly one tribe in Oregon that has a 100% rate of illness. They've had no live births in the past five or six years. Fifty percent of the Seattle Indians, urban Indians, have the same thing. So it seems to be, tragically, an epidemic among Native Americans. There might be a genetic tendency toward it, or we might be more sensitive, and then it takes something like an overload of your system to set it off. I'm concerned that there is a genetic inclination, but equally concerned that we are exposed to more pesticides, chemicals, and uranium than other populations.

I want to ask "How is this possible?" Instead, I ask if you see this as something writing can help change.

Yes. I'm currently at work on a book about this subject. It ranges from sections on the traditional relationship indigenous peoples have had with plants, to dreams, to the earlier smallpox epidemics, to memoir and family history.

Given all of what we've been talking about, recognizing all these things as facts of existence, what do you hope to get done in the next decade or so?

(Laughter) I think, what I'm doing now. I like what I'm doing. I've just finished a novel which will be out in April, 1998. I'm working on a new book of poems.

Hackberry Trees

We walk small
over the dry pond,
old bowl of the earth.
We walk over the fine bones of fish
buried in powdered silt
beside hooks.

This summer the turtle is gone,
pupil in the eye we called water
that watched us grow dry.

The trees are all that's left of water.
Beneath them the crickets
are sawing their legs,
dust for rosin.
Turn up a stone and they keep silent.

On the dark trunks of trees
shells of bronze insects
are open at the back.

We are like the trees,
they have been in this place so long
their yellow hearts could open.
The insects walk over our warm skin.
They think we are the earth.

Song for my Name

Before sunrise
think of brushing out an old woman's
dark braids.
Think of your hand,
fingertips on the soft hair.

If you have this name,
your grandfather's dark hands
lead horses toward the wagon
and a cloud of dust follows,
ghost of silence.

That name is full of women
with black hair
and men with eyes like night.
It means no money
tomorrow.

Such a name my mother loves
while she works gently
in the small house.
She is a white dove
and in her own land
the mornings are pale,
birds sing into the white curtains
and show off their soft breasts.

If you have a name like this,
there's never enough water.
There is too much heat.
When lightning strikes, rain
refuses to follow.
It's my name,

that of a woman living
between the white moon
and the red sun, waiting to leave.
It's the name that goes with me
back to earth
no one else can touch.

The Truth Is

In my left pocket a Chickasaw hand
rests on the bone of the pelvis.
In my right pocket
a white hand. Don't worry. It's mine
and not some thief's.
It belongs to a woman who sleeps in a twin bed
even though she fall in love too easily,
and walks along with hands
in her own empty pockets
even though she has put them in others
for love not money.

About the hand, I'd like to say
I am a tree, grafted branches
bearing two kinds of fruit,
apricots maybe and pit cherries.
It's not that way. The truth is
we are crowded together
and knock against each other at night.
We want amnesty.

Linda, girl, I keep telling you
this is nonsense
about who loved who
and who killed who.

Here I am, taped together
like some old Civilian Conservation Corps
passed by from the Great Depression
and my pockets are empty.
It's just as well since they are masks
for the soul, and since coins and keys
both have the sharp teeth of property.

Girl, I say,
it is dangerous to be a woman of two countries.
You've got your hands in the dark
of two empty pockets. Even though
you walk and whistle like you aren't afraid
you know which pocket the enemy lives in
and you remember how to fight
so you better keep right on walking.
And you remember who killed who.
For this you want amnesty,
and there's that knocking on the door
in the middle of the night.

Relax, there are other things to think about.
Shoes for instance.
Now those are the true masks of the soul.
The left shoe
and the right one with its white foot.

The History of Red

First
there was some other order of things
never spoken
but in dreams of darkest creation.

Then there was the black earth,
lake, the face of light on water.
Then the thick forest all around
that light,
and then the human clay
whose blood we still carry
rose up in us
who remember caves with red bison
painted in their own blood,
after their kind.

A wildness
swam inside our mothers,
desire through closed eyes,
a new child
wearing the red, wet mask of birth,
delivered into this land
already wounded,
stolen and burned
beyond reckoning.

Red is this yielding land
turned inside out
by a country of hunters
with iron, flint and fire.
Red is the fear
that turns a knife back
against men, holds it at their throats,
and they cannot see the claw on the handle,
the animal hand
that haunts them
from some place inside their blood.

So that is hunting, birth,
and one kind of death.
Then there was medicine, the healing of wounds.
Red was the infinite fruit
of stolen bodies.
The doctors wanted to know
what invented disease
how wounds healed
from inside themselves
how life stands up in skin,
if not by magic.

They divined the red shadows of leeches
that swam in white bowls of water;
they believed stars
in the cup sky.
They cut the wall of skin
to let
what was bad escape
but they were reading the story of fire
gone out

and that was science.

As for the animal hand on death's knife,
knives have as many sides
as the red father of war
who signs his name
in the blood of other men.

And red was the soldier
who crawled through a ditch
of human blood in order to live.
It was the canal of his deliverance.

It is his son who lives near me.
Red is the thunder in our ears
when we meet.
Love, like creation,
is some other order of things.

Red is the share of fire
I have stolen
from root, hoof, fallen fruit.
And this was hunger.

Red is the human house
I come back to at night
swimming inside the cave of skin
that remembers bison.
In that round nation
of blood
we are all burning,
red, inseparable fires
the living have crawled
and climbed through
in order to live
so nothing will be left

for death at the end.

This life in the fire, I love it,
I want it,
this life.

Grateful acknowledgement is made to Judy Grahn, for her lines in "A Woman is Talking to Death."

Crossings

There is a place at the center of earth
where one ocean dissolves inside the other
in a black and holy love;
It's why the whales of one sea
know songs of the other,
why one thing becomes something else
and sand falls down the hourglass
into another time.

Once I saw a fetal whale
on a block of shining ice.
Not yet whale, it still wore the shadow
of a human face, and fingers
that had grown before the taking
back and turning into fin.
It was a child from the curving world
of water turned square,
cold, small.

Sometimes the longing in me
comes from when I remember
the terrain of crossed beginnings
when whales lived on land
and we stepped out of water
to enter our lives in air.

Sometimes it's from the spilled cup of a child
who passed through all the elements
into the human fold,
but when I turned him over
I saw that he did not want to live
in air. He'd barely lost
the trace of gill slits
and already he was a member of the clan of crossings.
Like tides of water,
he wanted to turn back.

I spoke across elements
as he was leaving
and told him, Go.
It was like the wild horses
that night when fog lifted.
They were swimming across the river.
Dark was that water,
darker still the horses,
and then they were gone.

The Origins of Corn

This is the female corn.
This is the male.
These are the wild skirts flying
and here is the sweet dark daughter
that passed between those
who were currents of each other's love.
She sleeps
in milky sweetness. She is the stranger
that comes from a remote land, another time
where sky and earth are lovers always
for the first time each day,
where crops begin to stand
amid brown dry husks, to rise straight
and certain as old people with yellowed hair
who carry medicines,
the corn song,
the hot barefoot dance
that burns your feet
but you can't stop
trading gifts with the land,
putting your love in the ground
so that after the long sleep of seeds
all things will grow
and the plants who climb into this world
will find it green and alive.

Susan Ludvigson

The Heart of the Poem

*S*usan Ludvigson is Professor of English and Poet-in-
Residence at Winthrop University. She has received
*fellowships and grants from the Guggenheim, Rockefeller,
Witter Bynner, and Fulbright Foundations as well as from the
National Endowment for the Arts, the North Carolina Arts
Council and the South Carolina Arts Commission. Her
published books include* Step Carefully in the Night Grass
(John F. Blair, 1974), Northern Lights *(LSU Press, 1981),*
Defining the Holy *(Iron Mountain Press, 1983),* The
Swimmer *(LSU Press, 1983),* The Beautiful Noon of No
Shadow *(LSU Press, 1986),* To Find the Gold *(LSU Press,*

1990), Everything Winged Must be Dreaming (LSU Press, 1993), Helle's Story (Duende Press, 1995), *Trinity* (LSU Press, 1996), and *New and Selected Poems* (LSU Press, 1997) as well as a chapbook, *The Wisconsin Women* (Porch Publications, 1980). She has represented the U.S. at The First International Women Writers Congress in Paris, as well as at writers' meetings in Canada, Yugoslavia, and Belgium.

Ludvigson was born February 13, 1942 in Rice Lake, Wisconsin, the first of four children of H.C. Ludvigson and Mabel Helgelund Ludvigson. An only child for five years, she was joined by two brothers, Gary and David, and finally a sister, Mary Jo. Her family heritage includes Scots, English, Irish, and Swedish on her father's side and Norwegian on her mother's. First her father and later both her parents owned and operated small restaurants/cafes in Rice Lake, where her mother lived all her life and where her father served for many years on the Board of Education. Ludvigson remembers that when she was about ten, business problems forced her mother to work with her father as cook. In her words, her parents "worked terribly hard, but they were able to provide very well for us. For me, that meant having horses." She particularly recalls the joy of "Roman Riding" (bareback, standing on the horse's back, galloping) at the age of 13 and the subsequent embarrassment of being thrown by the same horse when she tried to ride not only bareback but bridleless. Ludvigson attended the Rice Lake public schools from 1946, her first year in a two year kindergarten program, through high school and then the University of Wisconsin at River Falls. She married David Bartels in 1961, and gave birth to her son, Joel Bartels, later that year. She graduated from the University of Wisconsin at River Falls in 1965 with a B.S. in English and Psychology. She received an M.A. from the University of North Carolina at Charlotte in 1973, and pursued further graduate work at the University of South Carolina, although she did not complete the Ph.D. Program.

By the time Ludvigson and her first husband divorced in 1977, she had worked from 1965 to 1972 as a secondary school teacher of English in Wisconsin and Michigan, taught in a special program for disadvantaged adults at the University of North Carolina-Charlotte in 1973, and worked as a mental health educator for Mecklenberg County in 1974. She began her association with Winthrop University in 1975, and during that association developed her love of travel and of France, where she hopes to retire. She married fiction writer Scott Ely in a small village in Southwest France in 1977. She affirms without hesitation that the marriage is one of the best things to happen in her life, along with buying an interest in a small house in France.

To balance the demands of her professional life, Ludvigson cooks and entertains, nurtures indoor plants, and frequently "begins learning to play tennis," a sport she with equal frequency abandons. Thinking of a childhood in which she was taught by her mother that "the most important qualities in a woman were attractiveness, 'niceness,' and the willingness and ability to keep a neat, clean house. . ." and that women should be "subservient to men" she credits her father with, perhaps unconsciously, encouraging her independence and (by today's standards) mild rebellions. She concludes that ultimately,

> my mother's values have had more influence than I like to think, and it's been and continues to be a struggle to give precedence to the life of the mind. Like many women my age who grew up in traditional families, I also tend to feel exaggerated responsibility for the well-being of everyone close to me, which takes an enormous toll on my emotional (and therefore my creative) energies. It's disconcerting to realize that I'm not nearly as free from my upbringing as much of my life would suggest.

You said once that you were an outdoorsey child, but that you also read a lot. What are your earliest memories of reading?

> Well, we had the kind of Carnegie library that all small towns had, in those days, with the children's section in the basement. They had somebody come and read to the children once a week, on Saturdays, and they had—I'm sure this was common throughout

the country — but they had a number of reading clubs, which were also contests. Whoever read the most books in a summer won some kind of prize. I never won the prize. Barbara Smith always won the prize.

A name that stays with you?

Yes! A name that stays with me. We were allowed to take out five books at a time and as soon as we brought that first five back we could take out more. In the summertime, most of the time, I would take about five every day or every other day. When I was reading, I was oblivious to whatever else was going on, and I remember my mother telling me that not she, but her cousin, was that kind of reader, who never knew what was happening in the rest of the room or the house or the world when she was reading, and who once kicked over a floor lamp and didn't hear it. That *could* have been me. I was completely absorbed in whatever I was reading.

What kind of things did you like best to read, in those 'competitive reading' days?

(Laughter) Well, in those `competitive reading days' horse stories. I remember reading the whole *Black Stallion* series — all the Walter Farley books — which I loved so much that I have thought about going back and been afraid to because I'm sure they won't be good —they won't hold up to my memory. It's like. . . my favorite movie of all time was *The Secret Garden*, which I saw when I must have been about five years old. Of course there's [been] a remake of it, recently, that's not bad, but my *memory* of that movie is just staggering. The images from it are still in my head. I did go back and read the book, and it held up very well.

Could you describe some of those images that have stayed with you?

One of them was of the wall around the garden and the children following the crow which picked up the key outside the wall. That's very clear to me. I'm sure this was black and white. My memory of it is always black and white. Then there's a scene inside the garden that the child must have been remembering of the mother swinging in the swing, and then the. . .Hah! Now I'm not sure I do remember, because I can't think what happens. I think the tree falls on her and that's when the father has the garden shut up. I also have an image of the little boy walking.

That's a lovely image — just the little boy walking. It's intriguing that you seem to remember the movie in terms of image rather than event, or narrative. . .

Yes, I did.

It makes me wonder if even at that point you were looking at things with a poet's eye as much as anything else.

I think that's possible! But in fact, I don't think I'm very visual. I think my *poems* are very visual, but there's some step that takes place that must be entirely internal. I'm always embarrassed about this, but I don't notice the world the way I think a writer *ought* to notice the world. I can be riding in the car with my husband, and *he* will notice all kinds of things that I don't see. Maybe partly because my eyesight isn't very good, but I also think I don't — I don't pay attention. Yet when I'm writing a poem, it's visual images that most often come to me. And I think I must be inventing them more than recalling them. I'm not sure if that makes sense or not.

How is it that you think a writer ought *to observe the world?*

Well, it just seems to me that a writer ought to be very observant, and ought to notice details of things — and it disturbs me that I don't. Or if I do, I do it in a kind of side-door way — which is to say I'm not conscious of observing them, but when it comes time to write, either I'm inventing (no, I can't be inventing) them —

Well, certainly not wholesale —

No, no. So it must be that they come back, but they come back in strange ways. But when people say that I'm a very visual poet, I feel a little guilty because *I know* that it's not from accurate observation.

When in your reading life — since we've embarked on sort of a history of your reading life — did you become aware of poetry as a distinct entity that's separate somehow from various stripes of prose?

Oh, I don't know. But let me tell you a little more of that history with the library! The children's section was very much unto itself and children were not allowed to go upstairs until they were twelve, so getting to be twelve and going upstairs was a rite of initiation — it was like kind of a biblical moving from childhood to adulthood, and I couldn't wait to do it. And when I got upstairs I started reading books that I don't remember the titles of now, but were considered adult books, that might have had just a tad of sex in them. The librarians didn't approve. And when I was in high school I remember that the scandalous book of the day was *Peyton Place.* That was when I was a freshman in high school, when *Peyton Place* came out. Well, I didn't know anything about it. All I knew was that a friend of mine wrote me a note in class and said "I babysat in so and so's house last night and they had a copy of *Peyton Place.* You have to get it! So I went to the library and asked for it. And I was chastised for even asking for such a book. And, you know, at this point I didn't know what it was. But then I knew it must be something I wanted. So I think I got it at the drug store . . .

That's where I got my copy!

(Laughter) Is it? You knew better than to go to the library!

I don't remember whether I tried the library first or not, but I remember buying that book.

Well, I read that book and I thought, *Hmmm. She couldn't have known much to write this book. Anybody could write a dirty book and make a lot of money. I'll write a dirty book and make a lot of money.* So at fifteen I made my first attempt at writing and it was intended to be the dirty book that would make a lot of money. I wrote about a page and a half of description of places that I knew nothing about, and then realized I didn't know enough about sex to write a good steamy scene. And that was the end of that first attempt at writing. At the same time, however, I was writing poems. I don't know whether I was *reading* any poems, but I was writing poems that were undoubtedly terrible — that were a kind of therapy, and which I was hiding under my underwear, and which nobody has ever read, and which I destroyed at some time. And so I don't have to be embarrassed by them — but there's no question that they would have been awful. It must have been when I was about fifteen, somehow, that I began thinking about words.

Therapy for what?

Who knows? I mean — being a teenager!

So was there a point then, maybe somewhere in high school, when you began consciously to realize that you were a poet?

Well now, in high school I liked poetry. Keats in particular. I always liked my literature courses. I don't think it ever occurred to me to write serious poetry at that stage. But when I was *teaching* high school — teaching high school English, I *did* get interested in writing poems but I didn't know how to do it and the only poems that I had read, really, were the things that one would find in the anthologies. One of the things that I did in my classes was to put a quotation or a poem on the board every day, for students to write about or not, or do anything with or not. We didn't talk about them. I just found things that I thought were interesting and I would put them on the board and lots of the students did just put them in a notebook. Every once in a while I would put one of my own poems on the board in place of the quotation of the day (never attributed to me!) and never had a single response. So I got no feedback, which must have been what I was looking for — for somebody to say "Oh isn't that interesting!" or *something* — but nothing. And I was convinced at that point that it was too late for me to write. It seemed very important to me to encourage students to be creative, and I did a creative writing unit (even though I didn't know anything about what I was doing) in these high school English classes. And I remember saying to the students very often, *It's too late for me. Whatever creativity I had has been stomped out of me by the public school system but it's not too late for you!* And I truly believed that. It wasn't until I was teaching in a junior high school, in Ann Arbor, Michigan, in the late sixties and very early seventies, that two things happened, really. One was that my marriage was beginning to go bad, so I really *did* need the therapy of writing, and I was doing that; and at the same time I had two colleagues who were serious poets. When I told them that I was interested in writing poetry, they took me to some poetry readings. . . . I remember the first poetry reading I ever went to, in Ann Arbor. It was Michael Hamburger. And then Donald Hall came and visited our school; he was there at the University of Michigan at the time. And he read Kinnell's "The Bear," which was, I believe, the poem that really started me writing. And it's *still* a poem I really love.

So then I began to take it just a little bit seriously. I was writing these, again, pretty bad poems that were really therapy. This time because my marriage was in bad shape. I showed them to these two colleagues. One of them was not particularly encouraging; the other was. And he said that there were two things I needed to do. We were on the point of moving, at that time, to Charlotte. He said I needed to write something every day *and* he said I needed to find a group of writers to work with.

Well I always tended to take advice very literally. And so I began trying to write something every day. And when I got to Charlotte, I did find a group of women who were just starting a workshop. And I joined it, and that's how it began — when I was about thirty.

When did you become a confident enough poet, in this chain of events, that you began submitting work for publication?

Well, you know, I *didn't* have much confidence. And my confidence is still very easily deflated. But in that first year that I was working with those women, there might, in the beginning, have been one or two who were writing poetry. Most people were writing fiction and non-fiction and they didn't know a thing about poetry. But they were encouraging. And some of them were at least on a level that they knew how to submit things for publication — they were publishing — and they encouraged me to do that.

The *first* thing I sent in — it must have been before I was working with them much, because I didn't know enough to use 8 1/2 by 11 paper. I remember sending some things on small stationery size paper. And I wrote a terrible poem — I wrote this with no irony — "To a Dying Goldfish." Which was taken by one of those anthologies that will take anything that's sent to them and the way they make their money is by having you buy copies of the book for all of your friends and relatives. But I didn't know any of this, so I was thrilled to death when it was published. And I got a long contract for it — (it was like a two-page contract for this poem — (laughter) but I was so extremely naive about all this kind of stuff that it was very exciting to me. Probably the most exciting publication I ever had, in fact. Then I got a little bit more sophisticated, but not too much.

Still, that first formal publication is a tremendous milestone.

Well yes, but of course we wouldn't want anybody to see that poem!

Well, we might, eventually, be willing. . .

No! We would not want *anybody* to see that poem.

Well, you know, you talk about having written a truly terrible poem, but I find that difficult to imagine. I can imagine clumsy, or. . .

No, I think terrible is the right word.

(Laughter)

But then I did get better fairly quickly. The first poem that "counts," that I think could be taken the least bit seriously, was published in the *South Carolina Review*. And then I had couple more taken. I don't remember where, but this was within the first year or so that I was working with that group. So I got pretty quick validation. And then I went to a writer's conference — my first writer's conference — and I had a conference with Paul Baker Newman, of Queens College in Charlotte. And as most beginning writers do, without knowing anything, I asked him how you get a book published. And he said *Well* — he took it very seriously — *when you have published about ten poems in magazines, probably that'll mean that you have about fifty poems that are publishable. And that's about how many you need for a book, so then you can start putting a manuscript together.*

Again, I took this advice *absolutely literally*. The minute I got the tenth poem accepted, I started putting together a manuscript. And I did have about fifty poems. And again I didn't know anything about the process. I thought — I must have known about *Writers' Market* — that must be where I looked. Of course it didn't have much about poetry, or if it did I didn't look in the right section, but what I thought was *I'll send it to whatever publisher publishes the most books.* And so I looked to see who published the most books, but not whether they published poetry. I can't remember where it was, but they didn't publish poetry. So they sent me back a note saying that they didn't publish poetry, and I thought *Oh yes! That would be something to consider.* So the next place I sent it was Princeton, which had a poetry series, and I got a flat rejection from them. Then I was going to Ann Arbor to visit, because I still had friends there, and I heard that Donald Hall was particularly encouraging to young would-be poets, and I thought *Maybe I'll see him there.* No, I think I didn't think that at the time. That was later. At the time I thought *I'll go to the University of Michigan Press*, that was what it was, *because they're there, and I know Ann Arbor.* So I called and asked them if they would see me. And amazingly, shockingly, they said they would see me, because I must have told them on the phone what I wanted to talk to them about. They were doing their Poets on Poetry series, and they did some things in translation at the time, which would have been early seventies, but they didn't publish contemporary poetry. I think it was while I was there that there was a big reading in the park and Donald Hall was supposed to read. I was going to speak to him then and then, as it turned out, didn't have the courage to say anything to him. So I went home and decided to write to him.

I wrote him a letter and I asked him if he would by any chance be willing to look at my manuscript. I had no idea what kind of imposition this was, or that people in the know don't do that kind of thing, but he was, as he is reputed to be, extremely kind. He handled it brilliantly, really, it's something to learn from. He said *I will be glad to read your manuscript. But I am so backed up with work that it will probably take me at least a year to get to it. But if you still want me to do it, I will.* Most people at that point would have gotten the point and said *No, I'll spare you that,* but I didn't. (Laughter) I said I'm perfectly willing to wait.

Ever the literalist?

Yeah. Ever the literalist. I'm Midwestern, after all. And so (laughing) in the meantime one of my friends in Charlotte said, *Why don't you send it to John Blair Publishers?* It was a small North Carolina publisher. She said *Mr. Blair probably won't be interested in you because you're not Southern, but they do pretty books and it's worth a shot.* So I did that. I wrote a letter saying *Dear Mr. Blair, You're probably not going to be interested in this because I'm not Southern but . . . .* To make a long story short, he took it. And it's not a very good book; it was apprentice work. It contained some of the very first poems I ever wrote, though not, at least, "To a Dying Goldfish," but really among the first things that I ever wrote. I've been embarrassed by that book for years, but it did open some doors. And so I can't really regret that it happened.

And after it was accepted, I did hear from Donald Hall, who gave me a wonderful reading of the manuscript, said a lot of nice things about it, told me it was very publishable. When I wrote and told him that it had been accepted, he invited me to come visit when I was in Ann Arbor at any time, and I did that, and so we've been correspondence friends ever since.

That's a wonderful story. And I'm intrigued by your comment that you've been embarrassed by that book ever since. How have you coped with that embarrassment of the early work that surfaces but that you really would rather not acknowledge?

Not very gracefully. I used to go and buy it off the shelves when I saw it in bookstores so that other people couldn't buy it.

That seems extreme.

It *was* extreme, and expensive, and I had to stop doing it.

Did you ever stop to think that they would put more on the shelves, and because of you?

(Laughter) Probably! But that's how I handled it. And I don't intend to talk about it much. And then, after I was divorced for a while, I decided to change my name back to my maiden name, and the book was published in my married name, so I was able to disclaim it without having to say much about it, most of the time. And now, thank goodness, it's out of print.

What do you consider to be your first real book, the one. . .

Northern Lights, which is the first one that LSU published. And I'm still happy with that book. It's not an embarrassment.

What changed in your work or in your working process between the book that you tried so hard not to acknowledge and the first one with which you are still happy?

Well, a longer apprenticeship, mostly. It was, I'd say almost ten years, well, no, . . . it was about eight years between the first book and *Northern Lights* and it gave me time to work on craft and to learn something about what I was doing. That should have been the first book, actually. I should have put in about ten years instead of two. (I *think* the first book was published about two years after I started writing.)

Then what you're saying, in essence, is that first book was really an adolescent book in terms of your development as writer?

Yes. Certainly. It would correspond to an adolescent book. It was very masked, for one thing. First of all, it just wasn't very skillful. I hadn't been doing it long enough. I didn't *know* what I was doing. And also, it was written during the period that I was about to get divorced — it was a time of turmoil in many ways. Not that turmoil is bad for poetry in general, but. . .

Then poetry must have given you a great deal, initially, for you to keep at it. . .and it must have cost you something as well.

It's given me a center. It's become. . .the purpose of my life. I think it's given me what religion gives many people. It's a kind of spiritual center. What it's cost me is, um, a lot. I'm still trying to deal with what feels like — this will sound melodramatic, and it's really not quite that extreme — but it sort of feels like the sacrifice of my child. My son was convinced, and I was for a long time, that I would not have divorced had it not been for poetry. I think that's not true, but I did believe that for a while. That if I had not become as interested in poetry as I did, maybe I would have stayed in that first marriage. Now I'm pretty sure that's not true. But the divorce was very hard on the child, and I think that I was self-centered and immature, in ways that were connected to the poetry somehow, and that caused him a lot of distress. And although he thinks he's recovered from it, I'm not sure that he has. So it's the source of my greatest pain and — I can't even say regret — because I'm not sure that I would have done things differently.

You've anticipated my question. If you were able to determine that in fact your child had not made the recovery he believes he has, would you be willing to sacrifice your relationship with poetry to change that?

I think maybe this is a rationalization, or maybe I'm evading the question, I'm not sure — but if I knew what I know now, I could have done a better job with him without sacrificing the poetry.

Is this that quality of hindsight that we develop, that shift in perspective when we survive events and get beyond them?

I think that this is a kind of corroboration that I am right. I think that I am a better parent to my stepdaughter now, in this relatively late marriage, than I was to my son. I give her a lot of time and energy that I'm conscious of, and I almost think part of it is a way of making up for what I did wrong with my child.

Are these issues of family, of family relationship, something that surfaces overtly in your work?

Yeah . . . yeah. I had a very early poem about the effect of my divorce on my child, and one of the most recent poems that deals with that issue is a very long poem that I think of as a kind of Faust poem. It's a poem that I've been trying to write for several years. I consciously wanted to do a Faust poem from the point of view of a woman, or with the woman as the protagonist. I'd made several attempts at it that clearly were not working and *I hope* I've succeeded in doing it this time. I have known for ages that's what I wanted to write about. I must have known in my core that the issue in that poem was for me that sacrifice that I think I made, the damage that I think was done to my son, for the sake of poetry. I wrote that poem — it has several sections — and never mentioned that issue. I can't remember how long, but it was long already and I thought it was finished when I took it to my poetry group, and they liked it but I could sense reservation. And someone said, rather tentatively, because they knew how invested I was in this poem, I think we're very honest with each other but we're also tactful, and one of the poets in the group, Julie Suk, said *I think you need to make it a little more personal.* And I said, defensively, *What do you mean, make it more personal? It is personal. It uses my dreams, it's got first person point of view, it's got this, it's got that. . . .* And they sort of backed off. And I went home and mumbled to myself, *What does she mean, personal?* And a couple of days later, I wrote that section, and it was so clear that *that* was the heart of the poem, it was what it had needed all the time. And I took it back, and that's what everybody said. And I think they even knew what it was.

That's a very telling phrase, "the heart of the poem," and not so much because it's one of those inescapable metaphors that kind of skirts the painful edge of cliché, but because it's a physiological metaphor. In writing about children, about mothering, its failures, its terrible poignancy, you're writing about a condition that is uniquely feminine. Do you see any other physiological connections with your poetry in general, or with that poem in particular?

Hmmm — I'd have to think about that.

Well, I can't help wondering about the possible connections with your surgery that year. . .

Ahhh! Yeah!

And writing times — particular times that you have set aside for writing over the years, maybe. It seems to me that there's a kind of female/reproductive mix in the creative process. . .

And maybe more significantly, and I'm not sure what this means, except that here's what happened about the surgery. I decided in the summer — two summers ago — that I was going to have a hysterectomy. I spent the whole first part of the fall preoccupied with getting the surgery scheduled. And all of this took a lot of time. But when I finally got it scheduled, I looked at the time. I wasn't teaching in the fall, which was partly why I wanted to do the surgery in the fall, and I thought *My God, I've only got a month left, and I've got no writing done! . . .because I've been spending all my time with this nonsense.* And a month before Thanksgiving, when I was having Scott's parents, and my mother for a week, so I knew that week was shot, and I had one month left, and I was just frustrated beyond belief that I had frittered away the fall on all this stuff. Well, I had brought back from France a book that I had been reading intermittently called *Holy Blood, Holy Grail* about a village close to us in France that has a number of mysteries associated with it. Very interesting place. I'd never heard of it, even though my house was within half an hour of it and somebody, one of our friends there, mentioned it to us that summer and said we really ought to go there. It was a village called *Rennes-le-Chateau.*

So we went and I found it fascinating and discovered that one of the mysteries, one of the legends of that little town is that Jesus did not die on the cross, (there are a lot of stories like this, similar ones) but anyway, he did not die on the cross, but crossed the Mediterranean with Mary Magdalen, that they were married, that they had children, and that either they or just she — they're not sure what happened to him, but they strongly believe that she died in that village. So I was intrigued by this. I had never heard the story. I thought I might want to write a novel about it, but I don't know how to write novels. I bought the book in the village bookstore, and it was about that story and much more. A number of interrelated mysteries but the main one is about a priest in that village who all of a sudden became filthy rich. He had reconstructed an old church there and when he had the reconstruction done, he filled it with all kinds of interesting puzzles. Sort of labyrinthine patterns in the floor tiles and various odd things, and there's all kinds of devil stuff. However, the authors of this book, after a long and circuitous kind of reasoning and reporting of their research, came to the conclusion that how the priest got rich was he discovered either the tombs of Mary Magdalen and Jesus or some strong supporting evidence for this legend, and was being paid off by Rome not to reveal it.

I finished this book at just about the time I realized I had a month left, and all of a sudden I got this *tremendous* burst of energy, and I started writing a poem that is called "The Gospel According to Mary Magdalen." A long poem. Obviously that story from her point of view. I was thrilled to death. I wrote the draft of it in about a week — not finished by any means — but I was writing a section a day — white hot. The experience was incredible, and I took the draft to my group and they thought it was good, and we were all excited about it, and I thought *Hmph! I saved the fall. I didn't waste it after all.* And then, to my astonishment, as the surgery date crept closer, I started another long poem. And that was the *Faust* poem. And I had most of a draft of *that* finished before I went in for the surgery. I am absolutely convinced that the surgery prompted those poems. That had that not been going on, I'm not sure what I would have written, but it wouldn't have been those poems. And so whatever connection that is, maybe I was thinking I would die in surgery or something . . .

Yes. I don't know whether our tape caught it, but I could hear it in your voice — there's a kind of finality in that "a month left" — which was a repeated phrase . . .

Uh huh, I think that probably I did. Rationally I didn't think that anything terrible would happen — but I think *irrationally* I must have, because I was panic stricken about that surgery. I *wanted* to do it, I knew it was going to solve some serious physical problems I was having and it did. I have no regrets about having had it, but I was scared. And it didn't have to do with — I think, I mean as much as one can know these things — loss of femininity or kinds of things that people sometimes worry about with a hysterectomy. I didn't think then and I don't think now that was an issue. I think it might have been mortality.

Which is, after all, the big one?

The big one, yes. For everybody.

You also had mentioned earlier that you felt for years that much of your creative energy was connected to your menstrual cycle.

Absolutely. And I know other women writers who say that too. Most don't. Most people don't talk about it. I didn't talk about it for years. But. . .

Why are you willing to talk about it now?

I don't know. I don't know. I guess maybe people are just more open about these things than I thought they were, or than they were. I even started finally talking about it in certain of my classes because I teach a course called *The Creative Process in the Arts* and to me, it was an essential part of the creative process. And it *does* worry me that I don't have that any more. What comforts me is that I see women writers who are doing their best work long after menopause. But the connection was very strong for me, and I'm still just a little bit worried about it. I have not been as productive since then as I was before.

Do you mean that there were specific times of the month that you came to designate as working time?

Oh absolutely. Absolutely. I had serious premenstrual problems and I was in a PMS state, usually for about half the month. And it was a terrible time for my life, and a wonderful time for my writing. It was such an extreme difference from the other half of the month, that I used to lecture myself when I was *not* in the PMS state and say *Now you know that you're going to feel differently in a couple of weeks. Don't make any decisions when you're in that state.* And then I would *be* in that state, and I would say *I know I'm premenstrual, but I think I'd feel the same way anyway. . .* and I'd make major decisions — some of which were disastrous.

There's a terrible temptation to say but, that's life. *Yet all of us — and I'm generalizing far too freely here — but all of us who are women, whether or not we are writers, make some major decisions that are sometimes disastrous and that very often are hinged to (or hinged on) hormonal cycles.*

Well. . .I do think that I made better decisions when I was not in that state. No, let me take that back. I sometimes regretted those decisions, but in the long run I'm not sure they were bad decisions. Mostly what I did was break off relationships with men. That was my pattern. When I was premenstrual, I would become convinced that something was *not* going to work, and that even though I knew this was not the best time to make decisions, I would do it. And then later I'd sometimes regret it. But, given the long view, I think maybe I was right. Those were situations and sometimes relationships that I'm better off not having continued.

What a provocative statement — yet, of course, you are in a second marriage which is now how many years old?

Not quite seven.

That's a substantial period of time. I can't help but wonder what happened that made commitment seem appropriate to you in this instance.

I hate to tell you, and a lot of women who don't think we are quite so much ruled by hormones will be critical of my saying this, but I have often said that progesterone saved my life. Not literally, I wasn't suicidal or anything, but it reduced those symptoms of that extreme premenstrual stuff so that I could make different kinds of decisions with more confidence. But it was more than that. Scott and I are very well suited to each other. He *is* the one. And I was ready. Readiness is a great deal, and part of my readiness was connected to beginning to take the progesterone.

This is just so intriguing, in a way, this sense of turmoil and emotional storm, because one of the things that illuminates your poetry, as I read it, is a deeply rooted serenity.

It's hard won.

*And yet the creative life that you describe is **not** serene.*

No. It hasn't been, though it's been much more serene since I've been with Scott. Infinitely more. The last two books should reflect that.

I think they do.

In fact, until I met Scott and made a commitment to him, I believed in that old ridiculous romantic notion that one writes best out of turmoil. And I think that part of what was going on was that I kept my life stirred up in order to be sure that I could write. Not for material, exactly, which is what some people would say, but that kind of tension in my life.

So then what you are suggesting, in some measure, is that you had become a poetry junkie?

Or a poetry-production junkie?

Yeah. Well, I wouldn't put it that way. But I do think I had things a little skewed. Yes. I suppose it comes to that. It was life in service of the art.

It was crucial to you that you be able to write?

Yes. Yes.

More than anything else was crucial?

Yeah. And I think that I designed my life so that by those lights — which I now think were skewed, very skewed — I would be able to write. But I was nervous, when Scott and I got together, that my life was going to be too tranquil and the energy for writing was going to disappear. But I think — and I could be wrong — but I think I've done my best writing since then.

What is poetry?

That's the hardest question of all and I don't think I can answer it. I don't even think I'll try to give a definition of poetry, but I will say that the poetry that interests me most is the poetry where I can watch the poet's mind on a journey, and it's an interesting mind that takes side trips I couldn't have predicted — and that there's illumination in it for me.

Are the writers who have influenced you most deeply other poets, or different kinds of writers?

Mostly poets. The first poet who influenced me deeply is Donne. And then Yeats, and after that more contemporary people, mostly women, but not entirely women, and I won't start naming names because there are so many, and the people I admire most change fairly often. I mentioned to you earlier that I think Rita Dove is one of the very best. . .

I remember that you qualified that with "If I had to make a distinction, I think this is what I would say. . . ."

Oh yes, yes. There are so many poets I admire, but if I had to choose one poet, she would be it. We were talking about Stephen Dunn, he's one. I think he's awfully good. I like Susan Mitchell a lot, I like Enid Shomer a lot. Mona van Duyn is, if not an influence, somebody I liked an awful lot fairly early. I liked many people. I was a big fan of Anne Sexton.

On a kind of related note, I remember growing up with a notion that the creation of fine literature, a fine poem, required a lot of time and contemplative space — oh, unencumbered time perhaps, images of the poet in his study, Dylan Thomas in his writing shack, perhaps — and yet it seems to me that an awful lot of very good poetry, very fine poetry, has been written by people whose lives keep them pretty consistently on the fly. And you, too, come to mind.

Well, that both is and isn't true of me. I *do* do a lot of things, but I also for the last seven years have had the fall semesters free. I made an arrangement with Winthrop that many years ago to teach spring semester and two summer sessions — the summer sessions in place of the fall sessions. And having that big chunk of time has made an enormous difference. I have felt that having that time was the greatest gift to my writing that anything could have been.

Maybe you can clarify something here. How is having that fall semester set aside in some way better than having your summer off?

It's a longer period. Summer comes to three months, and fall is more like four and a half months. Summer sessions are compressed. You can do a semester's work in a much shorter time. That's part of it. Part of it for me was, until recently, going to France for that period, where it wasn't just time, but it was physical isolation. We have this little house in a very small village; we know people there but not tons and tons of people, so that the telephone is not constantly ringing. The kinds of things that I worry about here I don't worry about there; I don't do the same kind of socializing, entertaining. And the isolation that the language creates is, in an odd way, useful. It may be one of my many rationalizations for not having learned French better than I have, but I think that being a little bit cut off by language is also useful for the writer. I am completely submerged in my own work, and what is outside is really outside. I have to make real efforts to speak French and to do things in that outside world. So inside my house is the place where writing gets done. And it works.

When I'm here, it's a little less effective to have that time. My time tends to be more eaten up with usual daily things.

How much time do you manage to spend in France?

It varies. I had just made that arrangement with Winthrop when Scott and I met. And at that point I had spent a Guggenheim year in France, and I had two more grants right on top of that — which is one of those fortuitous things — I had an NEA and a Fullbright to Yugoslavia the next year. So I spent three months in Yugoslavia on the Fullbright, and then the next year, using the NEA money, in Paris. So I had those two years together, and then I had a sabbatical year. In 1987 I came back from the sabbatical and made this arrangement with Winthrop. But Scott had just come to Winthrop, and that was when we met. They were not going to give him that kind of arrangement because he was brand new, and so he decided, because he wanted to go with me, that he would go on half time. He was publishing novels and had contracts for screenplays and we thought he could make up the other half of his salary that way. We went to France for three years, and we had his daughter with us for the first two of those years, and it cost too much money. We went into debt doing that and so we couldn't afford to go at all for four years. Now Scott is back on full time. We're still in debt, but we have decided to try to go in the summers. And this house that we have, we only own half of, in fact. I bought it with a friend in '83, and she just sold her half to Paul Zimmer and his wife, so they have it from the first of January until the first of July, and we have it from July through the end of December. So we don't have access to it really until the first of July. So the most time we can spend in it, for now, given that Scott is teaching in the fall, is maybe six weeks.

You mentioned Yugoslavia. . .did that experience (like France) have a lasting impact on your writing? And does it haunt you now in the light of present events?

I think all the time I've spent in Europe has influenced my writing. My sense of time and of history has deepened, become more complicated. Yugoslavia (and of course France) affected my whole life. A relationship with a man that began in Yugoslavia is still very important to me, both in terms of poetry and friendship. We travelled the country together, giving readings, meeting other writers, absorbing much of the tortured past of the place. But because we were in the throes of early love, the whole time had a kind of glow, even though we were aware of some of the tensions already building toward the disaster of the present.

You've written a poem for Radovan Karadzic, drawn from your acquaintance with him in Sarajevo, that has a lot of the "visual detail" you were talking about earlier — and it certainly reads like authentic memory and observation.

Yes, I tried hard to keep the "real stuff" in that poem because the history is so important. Normally I feel comfortable about changing details for the sake of the poem. I believe, as most poets do, that the truth in a poem is not necessarily tied to actual events; that the imaginative details are often more effective for getting at emotional truth than "facts." But the situation of the poem, Karadzic's relationship with us in 1984, when he was, as far as I know, not any kind of political figure, but a respected psychiatrist and poet, is such a bewildering contrast to the man he's become — a war criminal, for god's sake — that this seemed the vital material. When I see him in the news now, or hear him being interviewed on the radio, as often happens, it's always a shock. The man we knew in 1984 was (or seemed to be) a gentle, compassionate poet-physician. We spent a good bit of time with him in Sarajevo. The parts of the poem that are not italicized are based on real memories, and my intent is to suggest the disparity between what we thought we knew and what turns out to be a different "truth." More evidence for the thinness of the veneer of civilization, I guess, and the capacity for evil that exists in all of us. We felt close to Karadzic and still find it hard to imagine that he's the same person — even though, on an abstract level, we all understand that such darkness is a part of everyone.

Is your experience of Sarajevo linked for you in some way that isn't merely geographical with your experience and love of France?

Love is probably the key word. I was "in love" with Sarajevo — with a man and with the city. Even though images of Tito stared at us from every conceivable public place, an eerie kind of "big brother" presence, it was a romantic time in both the wide and narrow senses. The country was at peace, and we felt a positive jubilation at being there. Of course I feel that in France too. When my plane touches down in France, I find myself in grateful tears every time. I believe France is my spiritual home. I don't know why. I still struggle with the language, but it's where I feel most myself.

Do you anticipate being able, in the future, to spend more time in France?

I hope so. I hope that we can somehow get ahead enough financially that we can afford to take the falls, and go back again. And I'd like to spend at least half the year there when we retire, but that's a long way off.

One last question — clearly, teaching has been a tremendously important part of your life; your life as a teacher that has brought you from a high school classroom somewhere in Michigan to this office at Winthrop University — can you imagine a life without teaching?

Yes. I could. I like teaching a whole lot. I can't think of any way that I would prefer to make my living. I love teaching the poetry courses, I love teaching the creative process course, and now that we have this MLA program I teach a course called *The Intuitive Way of Knowing*, which is a kind of spin-off from the creative process course. It's great fun. I really love it. I tend to teach most of my classes at home. We do potluck dinners almost every class meeting — I love it and I love the kinds of students we get.

But, if I had all the money in the world, I would spend that time writing.

The Gospel According to Mary Magdalen

I. The Casting Out of the Seven Devils

Lord, I said to him, I sin.
What moves me to answer the flesh

when spirit calls in its light
and singular tones?

A well-made man is never invisible
to me, even beneath heavy cloaks.

Sometimes, as morning gathers towards heat,
a man's arm brushes mine in the market.

Then a bolt shoots through me like lightning,
the scent of earth rising around me.

What is this trembling, why does the wind
itself become dark breath on my skin?

I asked him these things.
I did not tell him that he

made my nights a desert where stars
were so bright they drilled into me

lying alone on the dunes. My kind of longing
was not his command.

I meant to do his bidding, though what he bade
passed through me like music.

Woman, he told me, I know you well.
Though devils spin you through lives

you cannot and do not wish in your blood
to forget, they are a gang of thieves

who will, if we don't throw them out,
take the gold and silver

your heart would leave
on my father's altar. They will strip

your walls bare where now
you delight your wakings with silk.

The rugs piled soft for your bed
will be rolled up and carried away.

These thieves will make you believe
the house of your body is aflame

and take everything
in the name of rescue.

Cast them out, Lord, I prayed.
Let me come to you rich with treasures.

His eyes described my being.
He took me by the shoulders, his hands

lifted me, and I felt the devils depart
all at once, my head in sudden pain

that left me so weak, I fell back
to my knees, weeping.

Mary, he said, so softly
I barely heard him. *Mary,*

as his hands stroked my hair,
as his hands stroked and stroked my hair.

II. The Anointing

I arrived at the house of Simon, a pharisee.
My master sat at his table, red wine

and lamb before him, the fresh meat
steaming, the fragrance of olive oil

a perfume of gold in the air.
I could not help myself, I began

to weep. I knelt before my lord
and let my tears fall, washing his dusty feet

in that overflow of rapture,
then dried them with my hair.

I could not speak, for his presence
stopped my words

as if they were stunned
with drink. I drew a small box

from inside my robe.
Opening its alabaster lid,

I poured ointment over those feet
while even the dove in the window

grew silent. Jesus loved
my penitence first,

then the way my hair fell
to the floor, its weight against his skin.

I kissed my lord's ankles
as if Simon were not in the room,

as if the other guests were not
exchanging glances.

Jesus laid his hand on my hand,
spoke to Simon and the others:

Try to understand, he said.
I have come for her as well.

My father never
blinded me to beauty.

She is a flame whose light
burns whiter now I am here.

And I? Look into my eyes,
black with awakening.

Even I must learn my way
by trial and touch.

The dove flew to my shoulder.
I felt its body hesitate, the tremolo of wings.

When the men spoke again,
only the voice of Jesus

entered my ear. I did not hear
meaning. It was like my own heart

beating wild, the sea
pulsing in, the tide rising.

III. The Wedding at Cana

I welcomed his mother into my arms.
Still young, she commanded her son

in a voice he sometimes rebuked, but she
would have her say. Though the servants

were mine, she ordered the feast —
goat cooked with mint and pears, spiced breads,

doves wrapped in grape leaves,
baked in wine, figs, an array of honeyed cakes,

and more. She saw to the cloths spread
on tables, hung branches over the doors.

She perfumed the house with incense and cedars,
that fragrance wafting to my room

where a girl brushed my hair,
braided it with lavender. Why was I afraid?

Bridegroom, I wanted to cry, to call him
to me. But he was welcoming guests

from Nazareth and from Capernaum,
from Magdala, my village, and from Gennesaret.

There were those who travelled even from Hebron
and Bethlehem, and from Arimathea

When I came out, some of the faces turned dark,
like poplar leaves in sudden wind.

So many, I could not recognize friends.
Bodies pressed back, making a path

for me through my house, now unfamiliar
as a foreign temple. But he took my hand

and when the vows were said, my heart lifted
and was glad. Then his mother whispered

that the wine was nearly gone.
She called the servants. Jesus said

Fill all the jars with water. When
they returned, it was wine.

Love, I said to him, I was water,
flowing over banks, flooding fields

already wet from too much rain.
You contained me. You changed me.

Which is the greater miracle?
More gentle than I had heard her,

his mother answered: He is the vine.
This is all we must remember.

IV. The Crucifixion

I was afraid. My fear was so great
the doves would not come to me

though I stood in a circle of crumbs,
arms extended, hands filled with bread.

I did not go into the hall
where the men ate their last feast together.

My lord had instructed me to prepare the tomb,
to lay clean cloths on a boulder,

to leave a jug of water there.
That night I watched the moon

cross over the garden, the moon with its placid
face, gliding as if through water,

as if it were breathing through water.
I wanted to absorb its white, cast

into the trees like hope, or to be absorbed.
I wanted to disappear.

When I was with him, I believed.
My heart's wings grew quiet. But away

from his hungry body, that body singing
its clear sharp note into the cedars,

I lost faith in the fragile plan.
There in Gethsemane, I tried to pray.

Nothing. Nothing but the rustling
of leaves, then a cloud racing to obscure

the moon, so that the garden fell
into heavy shadow, animals stalked

the paths. A wind came up fast.
Limbs torn from the olive trees

were cast on the ground. I ran, shaken,
to my brother's house. When Jesus entered

my chamber late with a lamp, I saw the bones
in his face, the wells under his eyes.

We did not speak with our tongues.
All night we were one voice.

       . . .

I could not watch them scourge him,
though I heard the lashes fall like hail

against his skin. I could not follow
close as he staggered under the weight

on his bloodied back. From a distance,
I saw him stumble.

Lord, Lord, I cried, What will become of us?
I was ashamed,

thinking of myself. I stood at the edge
of the crowd as they drove the nails.

Too far away to hear his groans, yet
they filled my throat, seemed wrenched

from my mouth. When the cross was raised,
I fell to the ground, lay there, I think, for hours,

while the crowd, restless, drank wine from skins,
stepped over me, laughing.

My fatigue was so great, I imagined the cross
had fallen on me.

At last, a shout went up. I raised my head,
saw a cup lifted to his lips.

My love's head fell forward.
It was over.

They took him down. I struggled up.
Someone helped me walk.

After that, I don't remember.
In my brother's house, I slept

until he woke me. Go, he said. Jesus is waiting.
I went to the tomb, my heart beating double.

I waited until the stone rolled back. Two men
in white attended him, two Essenes. They motioned me

to come in. Though he was weak, my kisses
were balm, my lord said, and would renew him.

I pressed my mouth to his mouth,
to his eyelids, then to his wounds.

His mother came in, and other women.
We carried him out into the sun,

which fell in rings
all around him.

V. The Flight into Gaul

In my brother's house we passed an anxious week.
The two Essenes stayed,

their white robes flowing quiet
through the rooms. The took turns standing watch

inside his door, those guardian angels. The rest
of us — me, his mother Mary, and my brother —

sat shiveh when guests came,
our grief not hard to feign in our exhaustion

and our fear. When we were alone, we gathered
grapes, salted lamb, put by a few clean robes.

One the day the Essenes proclaimed him well
enough to travel, we filled the skins

with water, packed bread and blankets.
By camel, by starlight, we travelled

to the sea, where my brother had arranged
our passage. The boatman did not know us,

thought us poor, glad to trade a simple fare
for the camels. He told us to be patient

while he led them
to a house in the distance.

Half a day we wasted, waiting for that man
to amble back. Even Jesus wasn't calm.

He rested in the shadows, watched the sky
his eyes ringed dark. I paced

beneath the plane trees,
keeping watch for passersby who might recognize

my lord. By noon, the air was still.
No leaf shimmered green to silver.

The few clouds maintained
their languid shapes. I fed my husband raisins.

His mother frowned as he took my fingers
in his mouth. I felt a shiver in my womb.

By then, the water was so calm,
I could see my face reflected, swollen.

At last, my brother pushed us off,
the craft heavy with the five of us.

The boatman, old enough to be my father,
rowed with the strength of two young men.

Our destination was Narbonne, a settlement
of Jews where we might live.

VI. The Branching

Between the pains, I remembered
the words of my lord:

The body, miraculous, rises
on blue wings, rises

out of agony and stupor so quickly
it's hard to remember the dark

paths of its going. It rises
shivering, then warms to stillness.

The body does not believe
in words, but in updrafts of air,

impossible transformations,
sun surrounding it, the whole skin shining.

Between the pains, I panted these words
and other litanies: Abraham was father

to Isaac, who was father to Jacob,
who was father to Judas.

I said the names, the charms
of the names, up to Matthan, who was father

to Jacob, who was father to Joseph,
the husband of Mary

of whom was born Jesus the Nazarene,
my husband, who came to be called Christ.

And Jesus, I murmured, is father to the child
who will be born here

in the city of Narbonne, in Gaul,
of me, Mary the Magdalen.

Lord, I cried to my husband, I am riven,
I will be delivered not of devils now, but of the son

of the son of kings. Flesh is made holy
in us. Once more and once more I cried,

as the pains came faster. Mary
his mother lay cool cloths on my brow.

Let us follow rivers back to their source, I whispered.
Let us cross white mountains into paradise,

into the promised land of the spirit.
Jesus prayed outside the room. He heard,

he listened to my words, my pleas.
He said, *Yes, we will go*

inland. We will enter new lands,
my kingdom will be cast, unending.

When it was finished , I rested, I slept.
I saw my image carved

in marble with a child.
I dreamed my husband's mouth

at my breast, woke to the infant Benjamin
suckling, the vine branching, the changed world.

Naomi Shihab Nye

A Necessary Act

*S*elf-described as Arab-American or Palestinian American, Naomi Shihab Nye was born in St. Louis, Missouri, on March 12, 1952, the first child of her Palestinian father and American mother. Her father, Aziz Shihab, was an importer and a journalist for The Jerusalem Times, The San Antonio Express-News, The Dallas Morning News, *and various Middle Eastern news agencies. His wife, Miriam Allwardt Shihab, graduated from art school, where she had studied painting, and became a Montessori teacher. Like her husband, she worked in various importing ventures. In 1956, Naomi's younger brother, Adlai Shihab (after Adlai Stevenson) was born.*

For Naomi Shihab, growing up in such divergent locales as St. Louis, Jerusalem, and San Antonio, education was an eclectic experience. She attended the Central School, Ferguson, St. Louis throughout her elementary school years from 1957-65, moving on to Lee's Summit Junior High School in 1965-66. Between 1967 and 1970, she attended high school at the Friends School in Ramollah, the St. Tarkmanchatz Armenian School in the Old City of Jerusalem, and Robert E. Lee High School in San Antonio, from which she graduated in 1970. Subsequent to high school graduation, she attended Trinity University in San Antonio from 1970-74, graduating *summa cum laude* with majors in English and Religion.

She married Michael Nye, photographer and "occasional attorney" in 1978. Their son, Madison Cloudfeather, was born in 1986. As a writer, Nye has found motherhood to her taste and advantage, an aspect of her life that has deepened her understanding and her connection with all humanity. Among her interests she numbers bicycle riding, walking, reading, talking to friends, "cooking up trouble" in her inner-city neighborhood, and "always food." All of these serve to balance the intense life of the mind required of her as a writer. Nye has worked as a visiting writer, in what she thinks of as "countless schools" since 1974, conducted poetry workshops with writers of all ages and backgrounds from rural to urban, middle class through poor, some with extensive formal education, others with considerably less and for two years conducted "poetry therapy" workshops with adults diagnosed as schizophrenic. She still serves as an occasional "visiting professor in writing" on university campuses in such locations as Hawaii, Alaska, Oregon, and Texas, does some magazine writing and indulges in what she calls other "writing-related" pleasures, including readings, talks, and editing anthologies.

The texture of Nye's work reflects a life filled with nourishing family and wider human connections, and with travel as well. She has visited both the Middle East and Mexico many times, as well as much of Asia — including Japan, Pakistan, Nepal, India, and Bangladesh. She has traveled and worked in Guatemala and

Honduras, and lived for two summers in Nova Scotia. Although she claims nothing more than that she takes her writing seriously and that she is able to "do nothing, very happily," Nye's impressive record of literary achievement implies both a rigorous discipline and tremendous appetite for work. She is the author of four full-length collections of poems, *Different Ways to Pray* (Breitenbush, 1980), *Hugging the Jukebox* (a National Poetry Series winner, also designated a Notable Book by the American Library Association. 1982), *Yellow Glove* (Breitenbush, 1986), and *Red Suitcase* (BOA Editions, 1994), as well as numerous chapbooks and *Words Under the Words: Selected Poems* (Eighth Mountain Press, 1995). Her first two books were selected for the poetry prize of the Texas Institute of Letters. She edited *This Same Sky, A Collection of Poems from Around the World* (Four Winds Press/Macmillan), authored a children's picture book, *Sitti's Secrets*, illustrated by Nancy Carpenter (Four Winds Press/Macmillan). Another children's book, *Benito's Dream Bottle*, a picture book illustrated by Yu Cha Pak, was published in 1995. Nye's editorial credits include *The Tree is Older than You Are*, a bilingual anthology of poems, stories, and contemporary painting from Mexico for children and an anthology co-edited with Paul Janeczko *I Feel a Little Jumpy Around You* (Simon & Schuster, 1996). Forthcoming from Simon and Schuster are *Lullaby Raft* (a picture book), and *Habibi*, a novel for young readers. The University of South Carolina Press published a collection of her personal essays, *Never in a Hurry*, in 1996.

Always concerned with the detail of daily life and the emotional weight it carries, Nye is a poet who finds poetry everywhere around her, as well as a prose artist who brings to her work keen observation leavened with humor and compassion. Writing, as she says, is for her a necessary act.

I always worry about trite beginnings, but I'm terribly curious about this. When you think of your childhood, what places come to you most strongly?

Well, St. Louis, because that's where my early childhood was, up to thirteen, and it was a very intense and very visual childhood. Then Jerusalem, where we went from there, and then San Antonio. I came here when I was fifteen — I guess that's still a child. And all three places were so utterly different that they all stay with me. Now early childhood, though — that's definitely Saint Louis, and the Mississippi and the whole feeling of gray gloom and red brick that is St. Louis so quintessentially. And I love it. It's hard for me even to fly through the airport there. I have a great emotional experience every time the plane lands and takes off again. I fly through there all the time, but the feeling never gets any less.

St. Louis is the setting for "The Yellow Glove." Is that a literally true story?

Yes. And the stream is still there. (laughter)

That's wonderful. That it should be true and that you should actually have found your glove.

And my son just had a parallel experience of losing his lunch box a month or two ago, and having it come back to him. Some boy reported to him that it was under the basketballs in the gym. He had caught a glimpse of its purple color under the heap of basketballs. *You ought to go check it out — I think your lunchbox is in there.* So Madison found his lunchbox and brought it home, and I said it was just like the glove (laughter). It's come back! Now his lunchbox has a new bouncy quality, like it wants to bounce through a hoop or something.

That's quite an experience. In "The Yellow Glove," you write about knowing there were tears your mother hadn't yet shed, and that you didn't want to be the one. . .

Right. Well, I wasn't about to cry over the lunchbox — although I am fond of it.

But did you get any sense of the same feelings in your son Madison that you had experienced as a child?

Yes. Especially when you write, I think, you become cognizant of the little threads carrying us along everywhere, tying us together and linking us up.

Did your mother ever find out that you had lost that glove?

No. (Laughter) When she read that piece, she said *What yellow glove?* She had no memory of it at all.

Kind of like "Making a Fist?"

Yes. She doesn't remember that either. But she likes the idea that she *might* have said that.

Sort of like the way we would like to be remembered if we had to be remembered?

Yes. Reinventing . . . but it was true!

And you went from St. Louis, with the yellow glove memories, directly to Jerusalem?

Actually, there was a year in between there — a year and a half — that I never talk about because it's complicating. But we did go somewhere else in Missouri first, and I was fourteen when we went to Jerusalem.

Well, now you've got me really curious about that "missing year" in Missouri.

That other year? Well, it was kind of a weird year. My father entered the Unity School of Christianity, which is in Lee's Summit, Missouri. He was working with the scholar and translator George Lamsa on a new translation that Lamsa was doing of the Bible. My father was helping him with his English, because my father had better English. That was our original link to Unity Village.

So we moved over there and my father actually entered the ministerial program. But he was not real ministerial material, and I could never understand it. It was almost as if he took an odd little detour. He was a great speaker, a very charismatic person, still is, and interested in studying religions. Coming out of a Jerusalem boyhood, he was interested in Jesus — though he wasn't Christian. His family was Moslem. He didn't finish the program. We left from there and went to Jerusalem. Our parents had been talking about going to Jerusalem — our move overseas had been anticipated. From when they married, they had wanted to live in both places, and I'm sure we would have lived there longer had the situation been more harmonious for us. For anyone. For everyone.

As an adult, do you miss Jerusalem?

Yes. Very much. I miss Jerusalem and I think about it. The book I'm working on now is set there, so that's given me a nice indulgent reason to think about it. This one is a . . ."teenager-novelito" I call it. Jerusalem is so permeated with layers and textures, minglings of all kinds that, once you've lived there you don't get over it. My grandmother died two years ago, twenty-eight miles north of Jerusalem. She was 106, and we were going over many times in the intervening years to be with her.

This is, of course, the grandmother for whom you wrote "Words Under the Words." Are those her words you quote in the last three lines of the poem?

No. They're just words that I imagined in her spirit.

Can you remember today what the words meant to you when you wrote them?

She was a fabulous talker. People would come and sit around in her room just to hear her talk. She would tell a story from 70 years ago as immediately and excitedly as a story from yesterday. So there was that sense that we shared the awareness of the abiding word — the words *under* the words. I would think about this when she looked at a page of print, as she did when she saw the book *Sitti's Secrets* in galley, before it came out. She stared hard at the words, and I knew that not only couldn't she read them — she couldn't have read them even if they were in Arabic, yet I always had the sense that she was reading everything. She could read everything—between and above and through and beyond. She had a penetrating intuition about things.

So that line, *Answer if you hear the words* under the words—I believe she did hear them. And I want to hear them. I've always wanted to hear them. She represented that to me. After I met her, I felt that I was always writing to her. Even though we didn't speak the same language and even though she couldn't really hear or understand anything I wrote, I felt she was present, not only as a source out of which one draws, but as someone to speak to, a listener. And she meant that to other people, not just to me. On my last trip to Jerusalem, very close to the end of her life, a man materialized at my hotel and identified himself as a Jewish anthropologist. He said he had gone originally to her village to do a project on Arab culture or something. My family had welcomed him. My uncle, Izzat, was the mayor, so they took him in and he rented a room, staying in the village a lot of the time, for a few years. He spoke Arabic fluently. He said he was so spellbound by my grandmother that after a while he had to give up his project because he couldn't be objective—that was the way he put it—in the way he had intended to be in the beginning. Then he told me that he had 2,000 pages of material—documented stories, things he had taped that she told in Arabic that he had translated into Hebrew.

And I said Well, can we see these stories? And he said But they're in Hebrew. And I said Well, I know a lot of people who speak Hebrew. Let's see them! And he said he wanted to give them to me, and then he died.

So now what happens?

My father and I are now in communication with his wife, wanting to get these papers whatever language they're in.

And whatever language they're in, you'll manage to read them?

Right. It was moving to me that he wanted to tell me *Your grandmother changed my life—the way she talked about the world and the way she looked at the world.* He went out of his way to find me and tell me that.

And then the unlooked-for bounty — 2,000 pages.

Yes. Which to a writer is — astonishing. I hope we can get them. I hope. He said *I'll tell you some of your grandmother's stories even your father doesn't know.* I thought that was interesting. How could he be sure what my father did and didn't know? So he told me some stories that, sure enough, I don't think my father knows. It was an intriguing encounter.

So when you met your grandmother, and even subsequently, you never really shared a language?

No. I only learned a very pedestrian kind of Arabic. She seemed as if she could understand me and we could get a lot talked about in our funny way, but she never learned any English.

Yet this was never an impediment to the relationship. How would you account for that?

I don't know. I guess it's a genetic mystery. Why are we closer to certain people in our family than others? I was very close to my mother's mother as well. I was closer to her geographically and of course we could speak the same language, while I was growing up. But we did not particularly share the same sensibility of the world, whereas with my father's mother, in some way I did. You know, you just recognize the people in your family you're most resonant with, and it's mysterious.

Would you say that everything wonderful is mysterious?

I would, yes.

Talking about your grandmother, Sitti Khadra, and language calls to mind another poem in Red Suitcase titled "Arabic," which is about a man who has invested everything, all meaning and all understanding, in one language.

I've always felt ashamed that I was not fluent in other languages. Since I've studied three of them, and live here in the Mecca of

Tejano Spanish, I might hope I'd be more fluent. Maybe some people just don't have a knack. I have a knack for accents, but not for vocabulary, apparently, or — I get the words but not the connective tissue. I've studied Arabic, German, Spanish and still can't speak any of them, although I can read, slowly, things in Spanish. And for a short while I could write very primitive things in Arabic, but that's lost to me now. It's as if I didn't exercise that part of the brain at the right early age, so it would be supple enough to be fluent. Still I think we can be infiltrated by the gifts of many languages, even without having a real grip on them for ourselves. I was intrigued by that fellow in Jordan who was so certain that Arabic was the key to awareness.

You respond to him rather positively in the poem, although one supposes it would have been easy to pull back from his stance, to say that it was too narrow and rigid. Yet you don't do that. You commend his wholeness of belief. Then you hail a taxi by yelling Pain. Why that specific word?

That's what we had been talking about, so it was the word uppermost in my mind, and besides, it was an experiment. I thought, well, now wait a minute. What if we call things by other names? What if you call a taxi pain? You put up your hand, you say Pain — it stops. Maybe things are more translatable than we imagine.

Well, as you say, the doors open in any language. The poem reminds me of Emily Dickinson's "Because I could not stop for death. . ."

"He kindly stopped for me."

I yelled "Pain" and he stopped and the doors opened. . .

(laughter) And I got in." That's right. I like that reading. I'm very troubled about fundamentalism. It's something I've become excruciatingly aware of the last few years, in *all* our countries, yet sometimes fundamentalist stances on odd things, like this man's stance on language, are intriguing rather than offensive. In India poets from state to state within the country write in English just

so they can understand one another. There are many ways. . . .
That's hard.

*Going back to your poems, your grandmother — who isn't bound
by language — is a woman, and the figure who has the rigid
alliance to a specific language is a man. Have you thought about
that at all? Or are they just different personalities?*

I haven't thought about that, but I have always considered
women to be intuitive, perceptive, expansive. . . .This is high gen-
eralization, because men certainly are too, but I think in these
poems, he's the one who wants to set things down and say *C'mon.
This is the way you should do it, and if you don't do it this way you're
wrong,* while she is sort of saying Well, whatever . . . *you know,
everything is everything.* So she's a more abiding presence. I did
think about this in the anthology *I Feel a Little Jumpy Around You*
that I did with Paul Janeczko, where throughout the book we
coupled poems by men with poems by women in duets. That
issue certainly came up looking at some of those duets.

*And what about "Voices," the poem where you describe language
as a plug?*

That was my maternal grandmother. *How could I know your voice
had been pushed down hard inside you like a plug?* That family was
very male dominated. The women followed along and did what
they were told. Although I discovered, in letters that were my
great-uncle Paul's, a letter from my great-grandmother to my
great-grandfather, saying *I will never never never never never
marry you!* And in the next letter they're married. So there's a
mystery there — that big gap. I haven't used the letters yet, but
I'm gong to do something with them because there's such a
haunting gap between what's told and what's not told.

And then that couple had seven children, only one of whom,
my mother's father, ever married. I think that's odd. Not one of
the girls married, and only one of the boys, coming out of the
mother who had said *I will never never never. . .*

I guess we're fortunate that one did marry. Else where would you be?

(laughter) Yeah. Well. That's right! A toast to Carl!

In another one of your set-in-St. Louis poems you write about a child coming to your house asking to "see the Arab."

Actually, it was two children who came to the door, and the girl spoke. The boy was standing behind her. My father was home — in the dining room. In those days, of course, kids would open the door for anyone, and he overheard me saying something, when she said *Is there an Arab here? We heard there's an Arab here. Could we see the Arab?* There was a long silence, and I said *No! What? What do you want?* I ended up saying *There's no Arab here.* My father came in and said *Who was that, what did they want?* and I said *To see an Arab.* You see, I really didn't think of him as an Arab in that way. I was little, maybe four or five. Then he talked with me about it. I had always known he came from somewhere else, but you don't think of your father as "an Arab."

How did you respond to the incident at the time?

I was sheepish. I was embarrassed that I hadn't answered them right. He was sweet. My father is a sweet-natured person, who laughed and said *Well, if somebody asks you again. . .* and talked to me then about what our name meant. He was never put off by people.

Yet it's easy to imagine that episode as negative, or at least unpleasant. . .

I met a dear woman a few years ago who has exactly the same background I do. Arab father, American mother. From similar parts of the country. Mothers from the middle west and so forth. We started talking about our senses of home. A difference was that she'd grown up more over *there* and I'd grown up more over *here.* But she said *You know, I don't feel at home in the United States and I don't feel at home in the Middle East. But I feel at home in both* places. So I thought about what a blessing it is not to feel alien anywhere. You know, I *do* see how it could go either way, and here was my counterpart spirit, for whom it had. She was always feeling shut out, and that people were always looking at her family as odd, herself as *other.* I had the opposite experience. I felt that I fit in everywhere.

You know, thinking about writing, the image that comes to my mind most clearly is children playing a circle game at school. As a writer, I may step back out of the circle and just watch them play and imagine describing it. Or I may step into the circle and participate. I never felt any compulsion to do only one or the other. I was interested in doing both. Having a family like mine helped me always be able to step out of the circle and look at where I was. I saw that as a richness, not a trade-off. I also felt close to other cultures, as I do here. I feel very close to this Mexican culture, and always have, because there was a sense of otherness that Mexicans must feel—do feel—in the United States, that I can identify with. It doesn't matter that it isn't my same culture. I've always felt that any little bit of other in our lives—even if its that we grew up on the edge of town and all our friends were on the inside of town—gives much more than it takes away.

That shows in your work, where the smallest details communicate that feeling. Where did your love of detail come from?

What else is there? I don't have an overwhelming sense of the universe, a kind of frame principle, a large world view or theory—I mean, I think about it now and then, and I'm *interested,* but details have always been the doorway by which we approach and apprehend the larger things of the world, the larger truths, whatever they might be.

My own lesson came in high school when I wanted to enter the National Scholastic writing contest in the essay division. I wrote two essays, one full of pompous high school philosophizing and one about a mouse which I kept as a pet, and the tiny movements of his day. He ate one single kernel of popcorn each evening. I was so attached to him I'd actually carry him in my pocket when I went to friends' houses. Then I told my teacher, *I can't decide which essay to send.* My teacher said *You decide that on your own.* So I sent the mouse essay and it won, which was a good lesson for me at a young age. The judges sent a letter saying that after reading a lot of pompous high school philosophizing essays, they were very thankful, finally, to have a sensory experience in an essay with a little mouse. They also said that the ideas the piece suggested were philosophical but implicit. That stayed with me as a kind of lesson that small things do have intrinsic and understated meaning that we need as writers.

Was that your first writing prize?

I'm not sure. I started publishing things in magazines when I was seven. I was actively sending things out through my childhood. In high school. I published quite a bit in *Seventeen* magazine.

And all that early publication experience was positive for you?

Yes. It gave me a common sense relationship with the process. No great mystique about it. People who don't start until later may worry more about being rejected. I didn't have any bad feeling about being rejected. As an adult, I dislike the language of writing — *submission, rejection* — but even as a child I felt *Oh well, they just didn't want to use my piece right now. Maybe someone else might want to use it.* So I'd send it somewhere else. I didn't think *It's bad.* By the time I was in college and knew that writing would be a major part of my vocation, I was at ease with the notion of not being accepted all the time. Why I sent out in the first place was never to prove that something was good, but to have a sense of connecting with people beyond my circle.

And I'm grateful to my parents for having been rather neutral about my writing. They were neither heavily enthusiastic nor critical. They would read things and say *Oh, that's nice.* Or *Thanks. I enjoyed reading that.* But they didn't make a big deal out of it — I've seen students over the years, who were good, be cowed by early achievements or their parents' enthusiasm for their "gift." But it was never that way for me — not that I had that kind of gift either. Because writing was a necessary act. People's responses were interesting or they were curious. But they weren't why I wrote.

Yet your writing works hard at connection — just look at your poems about your Uncle Mohammed, who lived on a mountain away from your family. Did he haunt your early years?

Yes. Because I was denied him, in a way. The person who's vanished is the one you really think about. I was very interested in him, and the fact that I didn't get to meet him when we lived there made him a little more of an obsession. I wanted to know him; there was a need to touch hands, to have him recognize me. My father was different because he was the only immigrant of his generation, but Mohammed was different too. He stayed in place and became offbeat.

He left without leaving?

Yes. He pulled out of the circle. So I was intrigued by him. My father did take that poem ("For Mohammed on the Mountain") up the mountain after it was published. He hadn't seen Mohammed in years, but he went up the mountain and said *I want to read you something that was written about you, and I have to translate it.* So he translated the first part and Mohammed snatched the book from his hands and took it, and said *I'll read the rest myself.* My father said *How? You can't read English?* And Mohammed said *It doesn't matter. I'll read it myself.* So he took the book, and my father stayed and they had a heartwarming visit. It turned out that Mohammed had been going down the other side of the mountain for years. I think he went by another name down in the other villages. My family, in their village — our village — didn't know that he was in these other villages, working as a carpenter, being with people — and it turned out his pulling back from the community had something do with an early love sorrow. Some under-the-table scandal involving him and his attraction to a woman — maybe something that wasn't appropriate in the culture. Then when Mohammed and his wife married, they had no children. And people hurt him by saying things like *That's what you get for your indiscretions.* I got this from the anthropologist, not from my family.

So you learned that he did have a life, and something about that life.

My father said he was charming, and took a whole stack of pictures for me. He was an absolutely gorgeous man. And then Mohammed sent me a present, a letter holder he carved of olive wood. So he knew we had a link. Anyway, it worked out.

What finally happened to Mohammed?

He was killed by a hit and run car, in Mecca, when he went on the pilgrimage, the *hajj.* He just had a tiny scrap of paper in his pocket, so it took months for them to identify his body. It must have been at the morgue on ice, or something. They finally tracked him to the village. He didn't even have a passport or anything, so no one could understand how he got across the border, where his stuff was, was he robbed after the hit and run . . . . Nobody knows. But finally my uncle had to go identify his body in Mecca. And it was sad for him, because he hadn't seen him for years. But I thought about it — Mohammed had been living this removed life, he didn't know how to cross the street. . . .

In some ways, it seems fitting that his last disappearance would be in the holy city.

Yes. And that his death itself would be a kind of vanishing. For months he was gone! He was lost! Nobody knew where he was. His wife was at home concerned as could be when he didn't come back on the bus. The bus people said *We lost him. He's gone. We don't know what happened.*

How did your family arrive in San Antonio?

Very strangely. Out of the sky. It was an odd place to land, and they really had no reason to come here. We left Jerusalem in a flurry at the time of the six day war. We went to Egypt, then to

England where my mother had friends. Then while we were there, my parents decided to take the ship—the Queen Mary II—on its second to last run. They bought a car in Germany, a Mercedes Benz, and we put it on the Queen Mary. My parents didn't want to go back to St. Louis because it would be anti-climactic—they'd said goodbye to everyone, *We're relocating. And here we are back again?* They were ready to try a new place. I remember them saying something like *Let's go someplace where neither of us has any history. Where we can just start clean and new.* So we're on the ship, and the ship publishes a daily newspaper, and someone has a *London Times* on the ship, and we're looking at it and there's a two page spread on San Antonio. And my parents started talking. *You know, we went through San Antonio that time we drove to Mexico in the fifties. It was a nice town. It was nice! It was warm*—We'd gone in the winter!—*Remember how cold it was in St. Louis?* and my dad said *Well, I know these men from San Antonio, these evangelists, and they were pretty nice guys.* I don't know how he had met them, but he said we could call them and ask for advice if we needed it. So we just came here. I mean, they didn't have jobs. They didn't have money here. They had no reason to come. My father walked into the newspaper and said *I'm a journalist. I'll do anything.* And they said *You're hired.* Then my parents looked in the paper and bought the first house their eyes fell on. I remember begging with them about that house, saying *Please, you're so reckless. Shouldn't we at least look at five houses? Three? At least two houses before we pick one!* It bothered me that they were just jumping into everything. I was as willing to come to Texas as they were. I just didn't want everything to be so random. To me it felt weird. But we moved into that house and that house is still in my family. It belongs to some cousins of mine now. So we stayed here. I finished high school here and my brother and I both went to college here. Neither one of us moved out—we both lived at home for college. So our parents would tease us sometimes—*Any possibility either one of you might ever think of moving?*

So San Antonio and the house turned out to be fine?

Texas was a wonderful, open-armed place for us to come. We've never regretted it for a second. I would defend Texas to the hilt everywhere. Certainly not all things about it, and I think San Antonio has some very serious problems with growth and "progress." But my parents were here eight years. They moved to Dallas when my father transferred to the *Dallas Morning News.* And I've been here — forever now, it seems.

When you bought this house, how many houses did you look at?

(Laughter) None. Just this one. We spent the first year of our marriage in an old stone rental house on Madison Street, which is where the name Madison comes from in our lives. One night we decided *We love this neighborhood. Let's try to buy a house down here.* We got on our bicycles and started riding around. This is the first house we looked at (more laughter)!

A family trait?

I guess so. I shouldn't make fun of my parents. An inherited trait — buy the first house your eyes fall upon, like the duck who follows the first thing it sees. Texas has been a great, uplifting place to be. I think we have a wide margin on the page here, which for writers is helpful. I have developed, over my years in Texas, a kind of claustrophobia elsewhere. I don't like being in crowds. I particularly don't like being in a forest very long, either.

Does that claustrophobic sense ever bother you in workshops or large readings?

No, because those are nice situations. It seems a great gift to talk about what you love and to get to listen to other people talk about what they love. That's a great gift.

Did you find that having a child changed your life as a writer?

Well, a child is such an enormous landmark—I think Ann Tyler said this in one of her essays — that it alters you in terms of your time, but you have so much more to draw on. You become a richer person. Having a child, for the first time, gave me a sense of being part of history, of what being part of an ongoing human species is like. I saw all people in the world differently. I had different empathy for people's situations, once I became a parent. And luckily for me, I've always been an early riser and an early writer—so I could always get up and work in the morning, before the baby was up. I never had the sense some people get that I don't have any time for my own work anymore. Not at all. You're restored to your most primordial experiences with language too. Our child was extremely verbal, and is still verbal. Now that he's in the third grade, he's becoming more of a literalist—and I'm this Daffy Duck mother who's not wanting to be literal at all. I profoundly miss the language of ages two and three, four and five—those early years and the boundless ways children describe things. As a writer, I think having a child is wonderful. In some ways it's made me more productive—being at home more has allowed more writing to occur.

When you write, do you always know when you sit down whether you're working on poetry or prose?

Not always. Lately it's been a little blurrier. I worked on what I thought would be a poem about the character, Pablo Tamayo, for two years at least before I realized *This has to be prose. That's why it hasn't worked out.* I couldn't get his voice into a poem, yet I had to have his voice in there. Usually, though, the shape is in the initial writing.

Is that "blurriness" connected with pieces like "Who's Who, 1941?" I want to call them prose poems, although I don't think that's quite accurate. In any case, the form of these is a box. How does that form come to be?

I'm not sure. I think I visualize them, almost, as I'm writing, as a box. I've got a whole book, Mint, that's a collection of paragraphs, and I call them paragraphs rather than prose poems. I like the shape sometimes (paragraph, box) because it's a humble shape that doesn't daunt some people the way poetry does. And it's a useful shape. When we're little we learn to write a word, then a sentence, then a paragraph, and so on. I kept waiting, after we'd gone on to the larger things, reports and so forth — I was waiting for us to come back to the paragraph because I thought it was such a fabulous shape. We never did, of course. You don't in school.

Many people don't in writing either. They never return to that humble box.

Right. That unit. I remember being very attracted to how the paragraph could feel so full! That it could be the whole pocket-sized story. So I wanted to play with that. I was already leaning toward that in some of the poetry books. You're right not to call them prose poems, really, because prose poems to me seem to be more imagistic, less narrative.

But these aren't really pedestrian prose, either.

I hope not. There's that blur between the two. But one thing I don't do is take a poem-shaped thing and turn it into a paragraph, or vice versa. Although there have been some instances where what I thought was gong to be a poem turned into a longer essay. But if I think about "Who's Who," which is a block shape, I know it was always that shape. I wanted it to look like "the block" in the block of information. I really love the paragraph. I'd love to do whole books in the future in that shape.

Do you have favorite poets that you like to quote?

One of my favorite quotes comes from Paul Durkin, the Irish poet, who, in a poem says *Could there be anyone who has not got mixed feelings ? Should there be anyone who has not got mixed feelings?* Isn't that great? And this in a poem where a woman has told him *I like you, because you seem to have mixed feelings.* And then he goes around muttering *Is that good? Is it bad? What does she mean by 'mixed feelings?'* He's asking an important question.

Does that illuminate your dislike for fundamentalist positions? The idea of a mind that doesn't entertain mixed feelings?

Sure. A fundamentalist mind doesn't entertain anything. It latches on, clutches on, to something, and says *Only this!*

That pretty well eliminates metaphor.

That's very interesting. Yes. I'm going to think about that. What a sad life that would be — a life without metaphor.

Or a life threatened by metaphor?

That's right. And fanatics don't ask the questions, and to me that's always been the most critical creative act. It's to ask questions, period. And fundamentalist minds don't. I guess they think they have the answers and so they don't have to ask any more questions. And so I don't trust them.

Maybe the fundamentalist doesn't have the strength for questions.

Maybe not. Or the stretch. The idea that you could stretch and come back to your own shape. That's threatening. And that's one thing that poetry can really give us — the sense of the stretch. That we can always stretch — poems help us feel that about our experiences. Fluent and fluid.

What would you say to the suggestion that poetry has become irrelevant to mainstream contemporary life — that it's become the province of academics who write for each other, who don't know (or care) about the lives of "real people?"

Whoever would say that must have a really lonely life, and obviously poetry isn't at any central place in their experience. Or maybe they're not identifying it as such. But I see it as not being that way at all. I think it's part of all our lives whether we identify it or not. The people who identify themselves as readers or writers of poetry are lucky in some way, because they're recognizing that what poems give us is something that we already have, and we *really need*. It's the ability to see, the ability to connect and many people are doing that in their lives, who wouldn't ever call it poetry. . .or. . .

Well?

I have this feed store just a few blocks from here called *Big Tex* that I go to, especially if I'm in a gloomy mood, to buy extra chicken feed so I can see the guys down there. They all know I'm a poet, and one of them is a songwriter. The other day, they were saying there wasn't any poetry in their realm, and I disagreed. So we got into a discussion of, oh, the click and clack of the feed warehouse, and how there is a real song and smell and sense and language. We listened to the next guys who came in — each one had the most melodious request for something — and we were just laughing. It was beautiful! But I've always felt there was a song right around us all the time. When people are missing that, they need to wake up. They need to *find* their poetry where they are.

If you could change something about the life you've lived so far, what would it be?

I would have been twice as alert. That's it. I really can't think of anything else. You know, you always have the sense that you could have paid better attention to little things. Really, I can't think of anything else.

And if, now, today, you could give your son one enduring gift, what would that be?

I think he already has it — the love of reading. The deep deep love of reading, and an awareness that you can turn to reading for so many different things, that it will sustain you, and be your friend, that it will do much more than just entertain you. He already has that. So I guess I would also wish for him — he also is a wonderful writer — the gift of metaphor, at this point, because I can see him as a young, very computer-literate boy becoming very literal, and he had such a gift for metaphor and description early on. I would hope that he would find that again and be charmed by it rather than put off. Just right now it may not be the closest thing to the surface.

And if you could choose something to carry you through, say, the next forty or so years, what would that be?

It's already been given to me. *Listening and passing it on!* I'm not one of those people who walks around all the time trying to feel worthy of all my life's gifts, although I know people like that and respect them. They're always asking *Do I deserve this life I've been given?*—I just don't think in those terms. *Pass on something good and you'll deserve it. You don't have to be perfect.* When I was turning forty, a few years ago, I thought a lot about energy. That was the issue, not age. Not all the dumb things that people want to focus on. To have a kind of vital sense of voice and story, life and word, the essential ongoing energy—I hope to keep inviting it in and not to be one of those people who goes to parties and talks about all the writing grants *you've* never gotten. Not to turn into one of those petulant, whiny writers. To maintain an energy and openness to what comes my way. That would be what I would hope for.

What scares you?

Losses. I think, sometimes, that it's amazing, looking at all our friends and our friends' lives that we're here. I'm forty-four, my husband's forty-eight, and all of our parents are still alive, and our families have not suffered any major tragedies, although as you know my father's cultural family, the Palestinians, have suffered so greatly. In our immediate family structure we've been gifted with a sturdy sense—nobody's a drug addict, nobody's in jail. . . . The world scares me, not close personal things. The world becoming stupid scares me. Feeling that we're at the end of a century and we're not very wise about some things. That's what scares me. Like in the poem "Shoulders," at the end, I say: *If we don't know how to do that with one another. . . .*and look how many places in the world we still don't.

Yes. As a testimony, almost, "Shoulders," which describes the tender bearing up of a child, appears in the same book with the poem to Ibtisam Bozieh. . .

Yes. And that people can still do these things to one another after pretending to be civilized for a long time now — that scares me. And of course in the United States, all the sad things daily in the texture of life. Like on Peter Jennings last night, the concern with what's happened to our sense of trust, and the mothers saying how all the things they did when they were children, things they wouldn't dare let their children do now, like just go ride their bikes for two hours. And that's what we *all* did growing up, yet the threats that seem to be present in society with poverty, over-population, drugs, crime. . . *everything* have really changed a basic mood. For a couple of years I worked in a mental health project here with schizophrenic/psychotic adults. It was very, very meaningful work. I did writing classes with them. They did them with *me*. Sometimes friends would ask *How many people are over there?* It was a day therapy center, so the number varied. Or ask something like *Doesn't it mean anything to you that so many people crack up?* My thought has always been that it's amazing that *more* people *don't*, the way they live their lives. I'm amazed there aren't ten times as many deeply disturbed people — because how many of us live rather threadbare lives without a sense of nurturing coming from somewhere, a sense of fulfillment or *voice*, or language. . . ? The kind of thing that poetry has given us, that writing and reading has given us. People who live without that, who live the kind of go to work and go home and watch TV lives. I don't know how they don't go crazy. I don't know how that would be. That scares me.

Do you suppose that it's living without joy?

Oh! So how can we continue to help — be tuning forks in some way? I guess that's the job of writers. We're tuning forks. We strike a note and it's not what we sing, so much, just that we strike this note—and then that note resonates in someone else's life, maybe they hear a harmonious note in their own lives. You know, *Where's that story for me? Where's the grandmother emblem for me? Where's the wise place for me?* (Rueful laughter)

Sometimes I've had people come up to me after a reading and say *Do you ever write about your family?* and I'll think *My God, where have you been for the last hour?* And then I'll think, *No, he was just tuning. I said something, he started tuning. He was inside himself and he didn't hear a word of this reading. But that's fine.* So then I'll answer him gently, as if he'd been paying good attention.

I have a personal mission at this time of my life. I really think our culture — our time — has been sickened by the word "busy." That word is one of the worst symptoms of our time. What it says about our lives, and how people consider their lives, is sobering. This is not to deny that we all have lots of things we're doing. But I think by saying that we're busy all the time we're negating experience at its heart. . . . It struck me one day when about nine women called me and every single one of them said *Well, now, I'm really busy but I wanted . . .* or *I know you must be really busy. . . .* That word was the one thread of every conversation. It's become a contagious code word of this awful supposed state we place or imagine ourselves in. If we really love poetry, it wants us to give up the word "busy" and feeling "busy." Now that doesn't mean that we still don't have lot to do, but we can feel differently about it. When I denied that word access to my vocabulary and language, things changed. . . . Just for example, nearly every day someone says *I know you're really busy . . .* and I say *No, I'm not. What do you want to talk about?* They look startled at first, as if I'm teasing them; then they slow down. And there's something in the way they slow down . . . when they're talking, some little different things happened. I think that we're denying ourselves experience if we are constantly casting up this smoke screen of busy-ness. Because then we're saying that we can't get to the thing that we really wanted to — but what is that? Have we lost it or let it erode? Who will we be when we get there? Each thing is still one thing.

So this is my evangelical mission. This is as fundamental as I get. We always heard when we were little that to read a poem we needed to read it slowly and we needed to read it more than once and to write a poem you had to pay close attention, write it slowly. And I think we have to live that way. We really do. There's a Thai proverb *Life is so short, we must move very slowly.* And I think that the word busy-ness finally just has to go. Busy-ness has to go.

Yellow Glove

What can a yellow glove mean in a world of motorcars and governments?

I was small, like everyone. Life was a string of precautions. Don't kiss the squirrel before you bury him, don't suck candy, pop balloons, drop watermelons, watch TV. When the new gloves appeared one Christmas, tucked in soft tissue, I heard it trailing me: Don't lose the yellow gloves.

I was small, there was too much to remember. One day, waving at a stream—the ice had cracked, winter chipping down, soon we would sail boats and roll into ditches—I let a glove go. Into the stream, sucked under the street. Since when did streets have mouths? I walked home on a desperate road. Gloves cost money. We didn't have much. I would tell no one. I would wear the yellow glove that was left and keep the other hand in a pocket. I knew my mother's eyes had tears in them they had not cried yet and I didn't want to be the one to make them flow. It was the prayer I spoke secretly, folding socks, lining up donkeys in windowsills. I would be good, a promise made to the roaches who scouted my closet at night. If you don't get in my bed, I will be good. And they listened. I had a lot to fulfill.

The months rolled down like towels out of a machine. I sang and drew and fattened the cat. Don't scream, don't lie, don't cheat, don't fight—you could hear it anywhere. A pebble could show you how to be smooth, tell the truth. A field could show how to sleep without walls. A stream could remember how to drift and change— next June I was stirring the stream like a soup, telling my brother dinner would be ready if he'd only hurry up with the bread, when I saw it. The yellow glove draped on a twig. A muddy survivor. A quiet flag.

Where had it been in the three gone months? I could wash it, fold it in my winter drawer with its sister, no one in that world would ever know. There were miracles on Harvey Street. Children walked home in yellow light. Trees were reborn and gloves traveled far, but returned. A thousand miles later, what can a yellow glove mean in a world of bankbooks and stereos?

Part of the difference between floating and going down.

The Words Under the Words

(for Sitti Khadra, north of Jerusalem)

My grandmother's hands recognize grapes,
the damp shine of a goat's new skin.
When I was sick they followed me,
I woke from the long fever to find them
covering my head like cool prayers.

My grandmother's days are made of bread,
a round pat-pat and the slow baking.
She waits by the oven watching a strange car
circle the streets. Maybe it holds her son,
lost to America. More often, tourists,
who kneel and weep at mysterious shrines.
She knows how often mail arrives,
how rarely there is a letter.
When one comes, she announces it, a miracle,
listening to it read again and again
in the dim evening light.

My grandmother's voice says nothing can surprise her.
Take her the shotgun wound and the crippled baby.
She knows the spaces we travel through,
the messages we cannot send — our voices are short
and would get lost on the journey.
Farewell to the husband's coat,
the ones she has loved and nourished,
who fly from her like seeds into a deep sky.
They will plant themselves. We will all die.

My grandmother's eyes say Allah is everywhere, even in death.
When she talks of the orchard and the new olive press,
when she tells the stories of Joha and his foolish wisdoms,
He is her first thought, what she really thinks of is His name.

"Answer if you hear the words under the words—
otherwise it is just a world with a lot of rough edges,
difficult to get through, and our pockets full of stones."

Arabic

(Jordan, 1992)

The man with laughing eyes stopped smiling
to say, "Until you speak Arabic—
— you will not understand pain."

Something to do with the back of the head,
an Arab carries sorrow in the back of the head
that only language cracks, the thrum of stones

weeping, grating hinge on an old metal gate.
"Once you know," he whispered, "you can enter the room
whenever you need to. Music you heard from a distance,

the slapped drum of a stranger's wedding,
wells up inside your skin, inside rain, a thousand
pulsing tongues. You are changed."

Outside, the snow had finally stopped.
In a land where snow rarely falls,
we had felt our days grow white and still.

I thought pain had no tongue. Or every tongue
at once, supreme translator, sieve. I admit my
shame. To live on the brink of Arabic, tugging

its rich threads without understanding
how to weave the rug . . . I have no gift.
The sound, but not the sense.

I kept looking over his shoulder for someone else
to talk to, recalling my dying friend who only scrawled
I can't write. What good would any grammar have been

to her then? I touched his arm, held it hard,
which sometimes you don't do in the Middle East, and said
I'll work on it, feeling sad

for his good strict heart, but later in the slick street
hailed a taxi by shouting *Pain!* and it stopped
in every language and opened its doors.

For Mohammed on the Mountain

1.

Uncle Mohammed, you mystery, you distant faceless face,

lately you travel across the ocean and tap me on my shoulder

and say "See?" And I think I know what you are talking about,

though we have never talked, though you have never traveled anywhere

in twenty-five years, or at least, anywhere anyone knows about.

Since my childhood, you were the one I cared for,

you of all the uncles, the elder brother of the family.

I'd pump my father — "But why did he go to the mountain?

What happened to him?" and my father, in his usual quiet way,

would shrug and say — "Who knows?"

All I knew was you packed up, you moved to the mountain,

you would not come down.

This fascinated me: How does he get food? Who does he talk to?

What does he do all day?

In grade school my friends had uncles who rode motorcycles,

who cooked steaks outdoors or paid for movies.

I preferred you, in all your silence.

In my mind you were like a god, living close to clouds.

And I wanted to know you, to touch hands, to have you look at me

and recognize your blood, a small offspring

who did not find you in the least bit

nuts.

2.

I wonder how much news you know. That Naomi, your sister
for whom I was partially named, is dead.
That one brother shot himself "by mistake"—
that your brothers Izzat and Mufli have twenty-two children
already marrying each other.
That my father edits one of the largest newspapers in America
but keeps an Arabic inscription above his door, *Ahlan Wa Sahlan,*
a door you will never enter.

We came to your country, Uncle, we lived there a year
among sheep and stones, camels and fragrant oils,
and you would not come down to see us.
I think that hurt my father, though he never said so.
It hurt me, scanning the mountains for sight of your hut,
quizzing the relatives and learning nothing.
Are you angry with us? Do you think my father forgot you
when he packed his satchel and boarded the ship?
Believe me, Uncle, my father is closer to you
than the brothers who never left. When he tends plants,
he walks slowly. His steps sing of the hills.
And when he stirs the thick coffee and grinds the cardamom seed
you think he feels like an American?
You think he forgets the call to prayer?

Oh Uncle, forgive me, how long is your beard?

3.

Maybe you had other reasons.

Maybe you didn't go up the mountain because you were angry.

This is what I am learning, the voice I hear when I wake at 3 a.m.

It says, Teach me how little I need to live

and I can't tell if it is me talking, or you,

or the walls of the room. How little, how little,

and the world jokes and says, how much.

Money, events, ambitions, plans, oh Uncle,

I have made myself a quiet place in the swirl.

I think you would like it.

Yesterday I learned how many shavings of wood the knife discards

to leave one smoothly whittled spoon.

Today I read angles of light through the window,

first they touch the floor, then the bed,

till everything is luminous, curtains flung wide.

As for friends, they are fewer and dearer,

and the ones who remain seem also to be climbing mountains

in various ways, though we dream we will meet at the top.

Will you be there?

Gazing out over valleys and olive orchards,

telling us sit, sit,

you expected us all along.

My Uncle Mohammed at Mecca, 1981

This year the wheels of cars
are stronger than the wheels of prayer.
Where were you standing when it hit you,
what blue dome rose up in your heart?

I hold the birds you sent me,
olive wood clumsily carved.
The only thing I have
that you touched.

Why is it so many singulars
attend your name? You lived on one mountain,
sent one gift. You went on one journey
and didn't come home.

We search for the verb
that keeps a man complete.
To resign, to disappear, that's how
I've explained you.

Now I want to believe it was true.
Because you lived apart,
we hold you up. Because no word connected us,
we complete your sentence.

And the house with wind in the windows
instead of curtains
is the house we are building
in the cities of the world.

Uncle of sadness, this is the last pretense:
you understood the world was no pilgrim,
and were brave, and wise,
and wanted to die.

Voices

I will never taste cantaloupe
without tasting the summers
you peeled for me and placed
face-up on my china breakfast plate.

You wore tightly laced shoes
and smelled like the roses in your yard.
I buried my face in your
soft petaled cheek.

How could I know you carried
a deep well of tears?
I thought grandmas were as calm
as their stoves.
How could I know your voice
had been pushed down hard inside you
like a plug?

You stood back in a crowd.
But your garden flourished and answered
your hands. Sometimes I think of the land
you loved, gone to seed now,
gone to someone else's name,
and I want to walk among silent women
scattering light. Like a debt I owe
my grandma. To lift whatever cloud it is
made them believe speaking is for others.
As once we removed treasures from your
sock drawer and held them one-by-one,
ocean shell, Chinese button, against the sky.

Making a Fist

For the first time, on the road north of Tampico,
I felt the life sliding out of me,
a drum in the desert, harder and harder to hear.
I was seven, I lay in the car
watching palm trees swirl a sickening pattern past the glass.
My stomach was a melon split wide inside my skin.

"How do you know if you are going to die?"
I begged my mother.
We had been traveling for days.
With strange confidence she answered,
"When you can no longer make a fist."

Years later I smile to think of that journey,
the borders we must cross separately,
stamped with our unanswerable woes.
I who did not die, who am still living,
still lying in the backseat behind all my questions,
clenching and opening one small hand.

Who's Who, 1941

I'm being insulted in a library. The librarian thinks I'm a high
school student sneaking out of class. "Who do you think you are?"
she shouts. We are alone. I want to answer enigmatically. I am the
ghost pressing against your window. I am the termite feasting on the
secret boards of your house. She stands, she glares at me. She has a
hairdo. The rest of the school is taking a test.

Some say everything is taken from us. A bowl is carried to the sink,
wiped clean, it does not remember who ate from it. Still we have
these moments when we remember what we never knew. A picture in
an old reference book looms familiar as a mother, a life story told in
neat clipped sentences is the life you might be living right now, in
the thin white space between lines. Will this be the year you do
something you remember?

"I am not a student," I say. I speak too clearly, like a translator.
"I am a student, but not the kind you think." She glares. It is
possible she truly hates me. And I place the book back on her shelf
as if it were a real book, as if those people pictured in the gray and
white 1940's photographs accompany me at all times, book or no.
Then I go trembling out into a world of rain, looking for them.

For the 500th Dead Palestinian, Ibtisam Bozieh

Little sister Ibtisam,
our sleep flounders, our sleep tugs
the cord of your name.
Dead at 13, for staring through
the window into a gun barrel
which did not know you wanted to be
a doctor.

I would smooth your life in my hands,
pull you back. Had I stayed in your land,
I might have been dead too,
for something simple like staring
or shouting what was true
and getting kicked out of school.
I wandered stony afternoons
owning all their vastness.

Now I would give them to you,
guiltily, you, not me.
Throwing this ragged grief into the street,
scissoring news stories free from the page
but they live on my desk with letters, not cries.

How do we carry the endless surprise
of all our deaths? Becoming doctors
for one another, Arab, Jew,
instead of guarding tumors of pain
as if they hold us upright?

People in other countries speak easily
of being early, late.
Some will live to be eighty.
Some who never saw it
will not forget your face.

Alicia Suskin Ostriker

And the Sky Doesn't Fall

Alicia Suskin Ostriker, whose work is notable both for its lyric intensity and its passionate intelligence, is the author of eight volumes of poetry: Songs *(Holt, Rinehart & Winston, 1969),* Once More Out of Darkness *(Smith/Horizon, 1971; enlarged edition, Berkeley, Poets' Cooperative, 1974),* A Dream of Springtime *(Smith/Horizon, 1979),* The Mother/Child Papers *(Momentum Press, 1980; Beacon Press, 1986),* A Woman Under the Surface *(University of Pittsburgh Press, 1984),* The Imaginary Lover *(University of Pittsburgh Press, 1986),* Green Age *(University of Pittsburgh Press, 1989), and* The Crack in Everything *(University of Pittsburgh Press, 1996).*

To her reputation as a poet, Ostriker adds her reputation as a Blake scholar and feminist literary critic. Her scholarly books include *Vision and Verse in William Blake* (University of Wisconsin Press, 1965), *William Blake: the Complete Poems* (Penguin, 1977), *Writing Like a Woman* (University of Michigan Press, 1983), *Stealing the Language: the Emergence of Women Poets in America* (Beacon, 1986), and most recently *The Nakedness of the Fathers* (Rutgers University Press, 1995), which combines wit and erudition in a brilliantly executed reconfiguration of Biblical literature.

Alicia Suskin was born on November 11, 1937, in Brooklyn, daughter of David Suskin and Beatrice Linnick Suskin. She remembers her childhood in various New York City housing projects as typically working class, except for being Jewish. Both her parents had completed college degrees in English, but her father worked most of his adult life as a Playground Director for the New York City Department of Parks, a job that his daughter remembers as "what kids called a 'parkie.'" Her mother wrote poetry as well as reading Shakespeare, Tennyson and Browning to her daughter. The family was enlarged by the arrival of another daughter when Alicia was ten years old.

From 1949 to 1955, Alicia Suskin attended Hunter College Elementary School, an experimental public grade school and from 1955 to 1959 the private Fieldston School, where she was a scholarship student. She completed her B.A. at Brandeis University in 1959 and her Ph.D at the University of Wisconsin in 1964. She married astrophysicist Jeremiah Ostriker in 1958, a marriage that continues into the present. The couple have three grown children: Eve, Gabriel, and Rebecca, as well as one granddaughter, Abigail.

Since 1965, Ostriker has been a professor in the English department at Rutgers University, where she currently teaches English and American Literature and Creative Writing. Like many other writing women, she balances the demands of her job and her family with her discipline as a poet and critic, two closely related aspects of her identity as a writer. When she needs to shift focus, she finds alternate ways of renewing herself by drawing, writing letters, and cooking; by her own admission she is prone to "raid the fridge" and enjoy hot baths. She also enjoys travel, and has journeyed to Europe, China, Japan, Mexico, Israel and India., citing Israel and India as her favorite "homes away from home."

Of her future ambitions, Ostriker says "I have been obsessed with the Bible and with Jewishness for about ten years. I wrestle with this heritage, and look forward to further loving contests with it. Women are transforming western religion — six thousand years of male monotheism will not be defeated overnight, but I hope to help." In reflecting on her life, she balances the joys of certain life experiences: "having sex, being married, having babies, the joy of teaching — against the shame of being an American during the war in Vietnam."

Describing her stance in the world, she relates: "I came of age, metaphorically, in the '60's, and have tried to retain the ideals of that period: the hope that we could have a more loving, wise and compassionate world if we would work at it. My feminism, like many others', was born in this period."

This backyard in Princeton is quite a distance from your childhood in some ways. Where did you grow up?

I was born in Brooklyn and lived there until I was six, then we moved to Manhattan. From the age of two until I finished high school, I lived in New York City housing projects: Red Hook houses, East River Houses, Dyckman Houses.

When people in the nineties hear the words "housing projects" they're likely to think of the worst possible experiment in high rise living, where everyone is constantly dodging bullets, stepping over junkies, in danger of violent attack — was that your experience?

In the forties and fifties, public housing was an experiment that mostly worked. We were in "lower income" housing, which meant that many of our neighbors were "on relief." What's called welfare now was relief then. Our neighbors were mostly Irish and Italian, with a small sprinkling of Jews and Blacks. Dyckman

Houses, in upper Manhattan was more of a mix. All these places were lively, rough, full of outdoor life. Kids playing every kind of game, the johnny pumps turned on in the street in summer, plenty of fighting. All these neighborhoods have deteriorated.

So you would not be likely to go back there, say, with your grandchildren, for a visit?

I still feel a pang when I drive by either East River Houses or Dyckman Houses, which I do maybe twice a decade. We moved my mom from Dyckman Street to Princeton because it was getting too dangerous. But there was no real safety problem when I was growing up, though I did get beat up a couple of times, and kids did like to take a smack at me.

Why was that?

That was because I was a wimp. I didn't hit back because I thought that hitting was wrong.

Do you suppose there is something in some kids that just serves as a "Hit me!" marker?

No doubt about it. And if the marker isn't there, they find out what a good target you are because when they hit you, you cry. (Laughter)

You wrote a poem, about a friendship you had as a child, in which you refer to yourself as a "lumpen" child whose friend was absolutely lovely.

I was the "lump-type girl" and my girlfriend Annie was a beauty! She was lovely to look at, delightful to know, and she had a really lovely soul. Otherwise she couldn't conceivably have been my friend, because I'm sure that I was a difficult, troubled little brat.

Moody?

Moody and broody. Surrounded by books. Confusing and confused. Annie was no reader. But she was my dear friend and I have no idea what happened to her.

Do you think that matters, in the long haul?

Well, I would like to know. She was a romantic. She had a sweet, loving, trusting soul. She probably married some bad guy. I like to think that sometime, by some accident, we'll meet. I didn't see her after I was twelve. I wrote about that relationship in the essay "I Make my Psyche From My Need" in *Writing Like a Woman*.

Did she move or did you?

We did. She came to visit once. I was twelve, she was fourteen. She made the trip by subway, something she wasn't used to doing. I thought she was coming to visit me, but my mother talked to her the whole time. And I sat there. That was the last time I ever saw Annie—and the first time I realized, there in pre-adolescence, that my mom was a space invader. That she couldn't tell the difference between me and herself.

After your move at twelve, did you need to face new schools?

Yes. Seventh grade was when I started attending the Fieldston School, where I was a scholarship kid surrounded by acres and acres of cashmere sweaters. (Chuckle)

At some point had you made a conscious decision to be a scholarship kid?

No. No, that was what I was to start with. We had no money, but my mom was determined to send me to good schools. And I loved to read. I loved school work. I was teacher's pet, which didn't help (laughter), didn't help me with my peer group. That was less so at Fieldston because everybody was smart. Everybody was bright. But I wasn't anything else. (Laughter) Yeah, I was. The other thing is that I was dreamy, in my little bubble.

You said you loved to read. What kinds of things did you read?

Oh, I read. . .from very early, because I learned to read when I was four... a lot of poetry, and fairy tales by the dozen. I read *Under the Golden Umbrella*. Did you read that?

Yes.

There were several Umbrellas, some of which were fairy tales and some were poetry. And *Little Women*, like everyone else. The first book I ever remember crying over. I cried when Beth died—I can still remember the phrase —"in the dark hour before the dawn." I remember Jo's poem to her dying sister, with the phrase "your prison-house of pain." Lovely.

And did you identify with Jo?

What else? But a little bit with Beth because I was shy, and a little bit with Amy because I was artistic. I drew all the time. And a little tiny bit with Meg because I loved boys. But mostly with Jo, like everyone else. As you are supposed to. And did you ever read *Rebecca of Sunnybrook Farm?*

Of course I did.

So did I. She was poor. So was I.

And she triumphed.

She triumphed, and I was going to triumph later on.

In retrospect, I guess we have to say "so you did!"

But she triumphed all the time!

(Laughter) Yeah. She did make a pretty consistent habit of it.

Every chapter! (Laughter) Never an enduring loss for Rebecca!

Nary a one! (Laughter) And from high school where did you go, on your way to triumph?

I went straight on to college. English major. I attended Brandeis, where they gave me another fat scholarship, and I lived in the freshman dorms for a year. Dorm life, group life, is not for me. So after the first year I moved to Cambridge with some other strange women. . .no, we were girls then. We weren't women, we were girls. We lived in Cambridge and I would get a ride in to school in the mornings and hitchhike back.

Innocent days, weren't they?

Um hum. They were. Sweet times.

Do you ever look back at your own college years and think, oh, not how wild you were particularly, but just how wild life is? that those years should now look like such innocent times compared with what we see in the lives of our students today?

You know, in certain ways they are more innocent than we were. They're politically more innocent. They may drink and do drugs and screw around, but they know less! They've grown up in front of the box. We grew up with our noses in books. Their common culture isn't books. It isn't even music, because pop music has splintered too much.

If I have a class of twenty-five students, and someone makes a musical reference, no more than a quarter to a third of the students in that class will recognize the reference. There was a beautiful stretch of time — the sixties, early seventies — when everybody's musical culture was together, and that was great. But now the shared culture is television commercials.

It almost leaves one speechless.

Well, it leaves something to be desired! (Laughter)

I suppose that ways of knowing and of processing information have changed a great deal as a result of this more video and perhaps even more electronically linked experiences, but I can't bring myself to make a judgment about whether this is good or bad. . .

Graduate students have an electronic culture. Undergraduates, at least at Rutgers, still don't, I don't think. Not a common electronic culture.

Was it at Brandeis that you discovered Blake?

It was at Brandeis that I read Blake's lyrics. And then I read "The Marriage of Heaven and Hell." Not until I had to decide what to do for a dissertation did I think about Blake again. And like a complete fool, without ever having studied him in a course, or even read past "The Marriage of Heaven and Hell," I thought, Well, I'll do my dissertation on William Blake because then I won't be bored.

Well, that's not really a bad reason . . .

Not a bad reason in theory. And I was determined, because that was a period when graduate students, at least in my department, would go around looking for some minor writer about whom not much had been written so that they could write something. On a minor writer. And I thought, I'll be damned if I'm going to do something boring that I'll hate by the time I'm finished. I'll do something interesting and challenging. And talk about innocence, naivete, being in a bubble. Without having read the prophetic books, I casually thought (laughter) oh, I'll just write on William Blake's entire poetic oeuvre and talk about his stylistic and prosodic development. Because all through graduate school, I had been writing papers on prosody and metrics. That was one of the things that most interested me about poetry, thinking about the music.

So you knew how to do that.

So I knew how to do that. So I thought, I'll do Blake. (Laughter) And then I sat down to start reading the prophetic books and . . . Ah! . . . I had never before sat down to read something I couldn't understand a word of. I thought I was smart. (Laughter)

(Laughter) It's so humbling when that happens!

I thought, you know, that I was a good reader! But I didn't ever read any more criticism and scholarship and all that than I had to. That was the part I hated. Literature was the part I loved. And here was Blake and he was literature and I was prepared to love him and I was not prepared to be utterly and completely (laughter) baffled by running into a barn wall. That was wild.

Were you already committed to a topic when you read the prophetic books?

Oh yes! I mean I had made my proposal and it had been accepted and I had my dissertation director, Helen White, who was. . . . Dear sweet Helen White, the purple lady.

The purple lady?

She was the medievalist at the University of Wisconsin, one of their stars. She always wore purple. A lovely Catholic lady who was the only person in my department who had ever written word one about William Blake. She had written a book in nineteen twenty-four.

And your dissertation was done in what year?

Nineteen sixty-four. She had written a book the object of which was to dispute Foster Damon's book on Blake and mysticism. Foster Damon says Blake follows the mystical tradition as defined by Evelyn Underhill in these five phases. . . and Helen White, who knew all about medieval mysticism said No no no no no! What he was doing was not mysticism. He was not a mystic. He was a visionary. That was the book. There was no way that she was going to be of any assistance to me at all in writing my dissertation, because she didn't understand him any more than I did.

Did she at least know something about his prosody?

Minimally, but the idea was that I was going to deal with the connection between matter and manner because that's what I always did. When I wrote about form I wrote about the connection between form and content. So this meant that I would have to understand the content. She didn't. I didn't. (Laughter) But I could tell that if *I could* understand it, I would have a treasure. If I could understand Blake, I could understand the world. Which was indeed the case for a while. I had the same sensation when I first started to read HD, which happened when one of my graduate students at Rutgers wanted to do a dissertation on W.H. Auden and HD, and I said W.H. Auden and *who?* (Laughter) Well, he threw some books at me and I looked at him and said *What's all this?* Then I began "Helen in Egypt." It was the same as reading Blake's prophecies, but this time I could recognize the sensation, and think: I don't get this at all. And I will. And when I do . . . Look out!

You know, even as late as Stealing the Language, *you were thanking William Blake. And you still are.*

Yes. I'm a better daughter of Blake than ever. I wrote about our long relationship in an anthology called *The Romantics and Us,* edited by Gene Ruoff.

Speaking of daughters reminds me. You once made the comment that you had gotten through graduate school by being the "smart daughter." Could you elaborate on that a little bit?

Sure. I was bright. I worked hard. I loved studying and learning. I loved literature. I more or less loved all the other things I had to study too. And I was the one who would wave my hand and ask questions. I never was a disciple of any teacher. I never had a mentor. I was a good daughter, but I was an independent good daughter. I never attached myself to a teacher. I tended to think I was a little bit smarter than they were.

Did they realize that?

I don't know if they did or not. The other thing I would do was flirt, which now is forbidden. Which is a pity. People flirt anyway, but now they're politically incorrect for doing it. Not me. I never feel politically incorrect. I just do what I do.

How, then, did you get from "smart daughter" to Writing Like a Woman?

By getting tenure, my dear. (Laughter) Tenure freed me to follow my passions.

Now where along the line, with all your love of school . . . you did love school, didn't you?

Yes! (Laughter) It was the only thing going for me. (Laughter)

So at what point in that journey from high school through graduate school to a tenured position did you start realizing that you were angry?

That is a very reasonable question. By the time I was working on Blake I already knew clearly that my affinities were with the rebels, the heterodox, the visionaries standing outside and critiquing the center. That was already clear and had been clear for a long time.

And how did gender become a real issue for you?

I think that was very gradual. It came about more through my poetry than any other way. Some of these formative stories I tell in *Writing Like a Woman.* Finding myself writing about the body and noticing that this was disapproved of; finding myself writing about pregnancy and childbirth and realizing that this was, for me, a set of experiences that were absolutely defining of my identity; dealing with themes that were as clearly significant as the themes of *The Iliad, The Odyssey,* and *The Divine Comedy.* Realizing that nobody, because these subjects were taboo, had written such things, and being simultaneously thrilled that I was doing something that had never been done. Of course it was being done by Sylvia Plath and others simultaneously but I didn't know that. How would I know that?

And in a literary culture, especially, that repressed the material you were drawn to. . .

Yes! And I was enraged at the wrong, at the injustice, of the censoring of everything that seemed to me most significant, that most deserved to be made into literature.

In The Mother/Child Papers, you started with a tremendous interest in prosody, a critic's interest, I suppose, to some extent. It seemed that in that book you were doing more deliberate experimentation with form, juxtaposition of unlike forms, and so on.

Yes. It was a very formative book for me. Formally, my two most experimental books are *The Mother/Child Papers* and *The Nakedness of the Fathers.* Those are the two books in which I had to think most about form and invent most.

In The Mother/Child Papers, what was the nature of that formal experiment?

First of all, the first section, which I conceived of as a prose poem, the Cambodia section, was working on implying a parallel between what America was doing in South East Asia, invading and mastering another body, exploiting another body, and what my gynecologist did to me.

The California gynecologist?

The California gynecologist . . . into whose hands I fell because I arrived in California seven months pregnant and I had to take what was there. Now I had already had two children with natural childbirth. Childbirth was for me a peak experience. It was sacred. It was like getting the gold in the Olympics and getting the Nobel Prize simultaneously. It was it! (Laughter) And this guy tricked me into having a spinal that I didn't want which prevented me from giving birth to my child myself. I've been angry many times in my life but never as angry as that.

Was there any outlet at all for that anger at the time?

No. Not a thing. I took my son home and shut up. I took my baby home, and the parallel was shiningly obvious. So that section of the book, "Cambodia," is a prose poem that partly breaks up into cadences, and then the next section is a section about mother-child bonding and loosening.

Do you remember writing the first page of Section II, which is so artful and so beautiful to look at?

<pre>
        was dreaming   be
  water   was   multiply
     dreaming   water   inherit

            in   earth
</pre>

Isn't it pretty?

How did you arrive at that arrangement on the page?

Between 1970 and 1980, when I was working on this book, I wrote everything in longhand before it hit the typewriter. So by hand, I did these shaped pieces on the page and figured out how I wanted them to look, and then worked on getting the Selectric to make them look that way. It was hard to do. The idea in that section was to go back and forth between the consciousness of a mother and the consciousness of her newborn infant. Though the mother's mind is clearly more verbal than that of an infant who has no language at all, still, the idea was to get at what is preverbal and to track the process from where the mother and the infant are a single, mutually responsive animal, to their gradual separation into two organisms, two animals not one. To do that musically and visually. That was the section of the book I worked hardest on as formal experiment. Then the next section of the book is really a gathering, a collection of poems written over a period of ten years under various circumstances. Those are more "normal" poems.

Yes. They look more like what we generally expect of poems short lines, regular left margin, plenty of white space. Was there any particular incident that triggered "Song of the Abandoned One?"

Yes. We were in Pasadena. Gabriel was born at Pasadena General Hospital. We were subletting, a very, very nice place with a tree house, a great hammock in the back yard, and a beautiful garden with calla lilies right behind the kitchen window. And Eve, who had been the baby until that point, went into a deep sulk (laughter) when Gabriel was born. She destroyed the calla lilies. (Laughter) Or at least some of them. Not that she said the words of the poem [Kill the baby]. The poem was my attempt to imagine myself inside the displaced child's consciousness. And my sense was that she felt angry and guilty in pretty much equal proportions. Guilty as well as outraged. Didn't care but did. Just like the rest of us.

Another of my favorites which also suggests an incident is "Propaganda Poem, Maybe for Some Young Mamas." That one seems to me atypically didactic.

I suppose it is (laughter).

Surely. "And if looks could kill I would have been one dead duck in that so-called feminist classroom!"

Well, I am a very didactic person. Let's face it. I try to control this, but I don't control it very well, do I?

In most of your poems I think you do.

Oh thank you, thank you. (Laughter).

I generally have the feeling, when I read one of your poems, that there was another ending that you "controlled" off the page . . .

Aha!

. . . so that the reader has to make her or his own leap into whatever understanding that poem is going to yield.

Thank you. My son-in-law said a very nice similar thing, which made me feel similarly flattered and loved. He was taking a graduate seminar in Contemporary Poetry in which everyone had to pick a contemporary poet for a presentation. To my astonishment, embarrassment, and deep *deep* pleasure, he chose me. And one of the things that said about my poetry was that it invited people in. Which I love. I love the idea that I write poems that are porous. That have openings and loopholes and. . .

Permeable membranes?

Yes! Yes! And invite people in rather than telling them something.

Truly, though, the speaker in "Propaganda Poem" was telling something about a situation in which that speaker was locked out.

Um. You're familiar with Coleman Barks. I have a couple of tapes in which Coleman and Robert Bly are reading Rumi. I'm very fond of Robert Bly, but it is an unequal pairing. When Bly reads Rumi, he's lecturing you. He's telling you something that you need to know. When Coleman reads, he's inviting you; he's seducing you. He's not telling you. And it works so well. And the contrast is so striking. It's a contrast of voices, but also a contrast of souls. And I would rather have Coleman's soul and Rumi's soul. It doesn't lecture at all.

That may be part of the soul's make-up, but it isn't always easily achieved. For example, when you were coming up the ladder the academic, literary, critical ladder . . .

My great shift came after tenure. It was after tenure that I, who had always thought I was a free spirit, became one. It was very liberating to me to get tenure. I took off my pearls. (Laughter)

Did you really wear pearls? To work? You mother must have been proud. (Laughter)

It wasn't my mother. It was my mother-in-law who gave me pearls. And I thought I was a free spirit, I thought I was a very independent type, but oh boy, when I got that letter, giving me early tenure . . . .

What year?

Sixty-eight. When I read that letter, very first thought, Phebe, I swear, was "Now I can wear what I want." Prior to that moment, I had no idea that I wasn't wearing what I wanted. I took off the pearls, I put them in a box, I did not take them out again for ten years. (Laughter) My skirts got shorter, I started buying funky earrings, beads. . . (Laughter)

How did the writing change? What did tenure do to that?

Well, I had not been writing awfully much because I had two babies in the house. So what did tenure do? For a while I worked on my edition of Blake. I was also writing poems. The poems were getting rather more free. . .but I was totally, totally saturated in Blake, while I was doing the Penguin Blake. Then, when I picked my head up from that project I started reading women's poetry, devouring women's poetry, said I want to teach this!, started teaching it, started writing about it. . . . I could never have done that if I hadn't been tenured. I wouldn't have had the nerve, because I'm a very shy and fearful person. It's true.

I understand that. So feminism must have been an astonishing thing, an astonishingly potent thing, if I can use that adjective.

Do we have a female equivalent of "potent?" We do not.

I like to think we can just take theirs and they can find another one.

(Laughter) Oh. Yeah. Potent. Yes. Of course. It was very powerful for me. And I'm not an organizational person. I went to a couple of consciousness raising sessions . . .

But you didn't even like dorms! How did you manage . . .

Well, so I didn't do that route. I became a feminist through poetry. It was instantly clear to me—the more I read the more clear it was, that women's poetry was as revolutionary as anything that had come up the turnpike since early modernism, and that it was a collective noise, sound, chorale of voices that I was hearing. And simultaneously, my critical head was asking: What is happening? What is that collective voice saying that has never been said in the history of poetry? I mean that was very clear. *Something's happening here, and you don't know what it is, do you, Honey?* But we're all hearing it. It's in the bloodstream, it's in the air. What is it? And that was what produced *Stealing the Language.* I figured that out. What is it!?

So, what is it?

It's all the things I try to describe in *Stealing the Language* (laughter)—ways of talking about identity, about the body, about anger, and about love, and about history and narrative. How we perceive, how we conceive, what we understand reality to be.

Given that, the revolutionary body of work, the concert of voices, it wasn't just Sylvia and Anne, or maybe Marge. This was a vast legion of voices. How has that, just going back twenty or thirty years, changed American poetry in the nineties?

I guess the most obvious way that women's poetry has changed American poetry is that it frees men to do some of the things that women do. To write more freely and intimately about their bodies, their feelings, their children.

Robert Hass comes to mind—those wonderful, personal, man's poems that I could not have read as an undergraduate because no one was writing them.

And that he could not have written before the women's movement. That no man could have written before the women's movement, except Whitman and Allen Ginsberg, but they were gay. When I started reading women's poetry in huge masses, it not only aroused my critical consciousness; it was speaking to me personally, in a way that no poetry had ever quite done before. This was hugely exhilarating and exciting and extremely painful. It changed me. And changed my work.

Is this how you moved beyond the almost plaintive indictment in **The Mother/Child Papers?** *There's a sense of desperation in that book, anger too, but a sense of having run into a wall. . .*

That's interesting. I guess that's right.

For instance, in the very last poem, the dream poem, you close with the woman giving birth "for the duration of this dream" and I wanted it to end with duration, for as long as she is not for the duration of a dream, which seems rather ephemeral . . .

What did I mean in that final poem? I saw that as a collective dream, by and of, the goddess. So the duration of the dream is the duration of human history.

Interesting. Because my tendency is to read that as purely a personal dream. . .making my own leap to understanding, I suppose.

But it is that also.

Have you ever felt that feminism failed you?

That's a hard question because there are so many feminisms. Academic theoretical feminism has become increasingly abstract and dependent on male authority. The feminism which needs to cite Lacan or Heidegger is a feminism that has severed itself from its roots in women's lives. On the other hand, Women's Studies feminism seems to be increasingly anti-intellectual. There is nothing there but opposition to the canon, white male. . .

Sort of a "get the guys" feminism?

It's get the guys, but it's also get the white girls, get the heterosexual girls. . . , it's the feminism which is rooted in victimization and which is anti-intellectual because men are intellectual. That's the equal and opposite mistake, I think. There is a reason why your typical American eighteen-year-old or your typical American thirty-five-year-old will say *Of course I believe in equal pay for equal work, but I'm not a feminist.*

I find that sort of statement unnerving. Every time I hear it, it scares me to death.

But why is it? Why, if the question is asked, will feminism be repudiated, rejected? Partly it's the hatchet work of the media backlash, but partly it's because academic feminists are not seeing it as their responsibility or obligation to address themselves to the real lives of all women.

Where do you suppose that will lead?

In the theoretical branch, it leads to academic business-as-usual. You learn to speak a certain kind of language, imitate a master discourse and the fact that it's a feminist master discourse doesn't differentiate it from other master discourses, and then, you know, you win/you're in.

Except that you haven't really won and you aren't really in.

Well, it's pretty hot academically right now. If you win a job, if you win tenure, that's a pretty big thing to win. A pretty satisfying thing to be in.

But does anyone take that discourse seriously outside of that discourse?

It doesn't change the world. It's not designed to. It's designed to get you tenure and make you feel good about yourself.

(Laughter)

Okay. That's a nice loop; but it is a loop. And if feminism doesn't address real lives of real women. . .well, that's a serious disjunction. And maybe it relates to two other subjects I was hoping we could discuss. One is rape and the other is mastectomy.

No problem!

Then let me start by admitting that I haven't read every word you've written, but I've done pretty well. The only reference that I have been able to find in your poems to having been raped is in "In the 25th Year of Marriage It Goes On." And it's almost a glancing reference.

Yes. The poem is very oblique. It's a poem about a marital fight, the trigger of which was that I had been raped by someone who broke into my home. About ten years later my husband said he'd rather have died than have had me be raped, which made me totally furious. (Laughter) I wanted to kill him. What a stupid thing to say. I wrote about the rape in a prose piece which was published in *The Village Voice,* then later in *Cosmopolitan.* I didn't use my own name. Writing it was very easy. I did it on a plane from Newark to California. Five hours. Boom! Finished piece. No sweat at all. The sweat was deciding whether or not to read it to my writers' co-op, US1. That was really hard because I was terrified. We're talking about 1974. . .and I was truly terrified that since some of the people knew that this had happened to me, and some did not, I could read the piece and everybody could be silent and change the subject and not want to be friends with me ever again. But it didn't happen. I had to take that risk. And bless them, when I read it, they talked about the form, they talked about the content. They were there for me, as the saying goes.

Which is what a workshop should do?

Which is what a workshop should do. Their response was tremendously reassuring. And after it appeared in print, *The Voice* asked me to respond to a letter to the editor that said I deserved to be raped because I hadn't fought. Now, my rapist was a man with a six inch knife, who must have weighed about 250 pounds. Fight? Ha. What I wanted was to stay alive. So they printed that letter and my rebuttal, which was written very compactly and with a white heat. And then I thought, well, I'm really finished with this. Until about ten years later, I found myself speaking in an undergraduate class about having been raped and realized that I had not done so before. I thought, *Ah, you never know just how unfree you are until you take that next step.*

Like the pearls?

Like the pearls.

In American culture as I understand it and as I have experienced it, for a woman to speak publicly about her own rape is a project heavy with risk.

But of course that's nonsense.

Perhaps, but it's nonsense we've all been steeped in from babyhood—and have carried with us every step of the way.

But still, it is nonsense. And like other things that you don't know you're afraid of doing until you do them, and realize that you haven't done them before. And the sky doesn't fall, but in fact you get points for it. (Laughter) It was like that. I was not ever aware of being cowardly before, but when I did speak of being raped to an undergraduate class, at the moment that I did, I was conscious I'd been cowardly for ten years, and simultaneously the consequence was that the students loved it. They were so grateful! Oh! This is something that can be talked about instead of something that can't be talked about.

That's a big thing.

It's a tremendous thing. What I try to do in all of my work, in my poetry, in my prose, in my teaching, is try insofar as I can, to operate on the principle of killing the censor and bringing what's supposed to be kept unconscious into consciousness. Discover what is supposed to be silenced and bring it out into the open, into language.

That effort underpins "The Mastectomy Poems" as well. What strain did the process of dealing with breast cancer create in your personal, creative, professional life?

Interestingly . . . it was a difficult and frightening experience, as was being raped and overcoming the shame of being raped by force of will. I should say about being raped that I set my mind on recovery and had a very, very clear sense of what recovery meant. It meant that every time some detrimental, slimy, self-hating thought would arise, like a plant in a swamp — which was all the time because a rape victim feels disgusting and defiled and slimy and evil and bad — I had to stop it consciously. So part of the work was being very alert and whenever a fiber of self-hatred started unfurling itself, wanting to twine itself around me like a vine, I'd catch it, you know, an inch above the ground and snip it as best I could. It took a lot of work, a lot of concentrated energy, for several months. I also had a specific set of psychological goals. I wanted to not have my love of my body changed, to not have my enjoyment of sex changed, and to not have my feelings toward black people changed because the rapist was a black guy. That was what I aimed at and that was where I arrived. The cost was that I was very self-absorbed during that whole period of self- therapy. And the permanent loss was that I ended up more self-protective, more armored, than I had been before or than I wanted to be. And then what happened twenty years later . . . .

The breast cancer diagnosis . . .

. . . was a lot easier, actually, less traumatic. It was very, very difficult. It was very, very frightening. But I think I recovered faster. My family was more help. The whole thing was less taboo and therefore it was easier for my family and for friends to be supportive. Or maybe I was just older and wiser and more able to allow people to help me. I didn't feel that I had to do it all by myself. Writing the mastectomy poems was just fun. That shouldn't have been the case, but it was the case. It was fun to write those poems. I knew I had a very good juicy hunk of material that was worth working on, that was worth bringing from incoherent, terrifying experience into form, and that if I worked really hard I could do it.

That sounds like art as personal effort and personal reward, but surely art is something more than that. What is it that art does in the world?

What art does is always invisible. It comes from the psyche of the artist, it goes to the psyche of the reader, the viewer, the audience. It acts silently and invisibly, as teaching does. You don't see the result when you're teaching. Or as parenting does. You don't expect gratitude. (Laughter) Or if you do, well . . . . As an artist you're always gambling. Your gamble is that your secret will speak to the secrets of others, that your truth will speak to the truths of others and will re-enforce their own reality to them, make them stronger. Seriously, poetry is doing very well right now. Poetry doesn't sell the way the fiction sells, but the people who buy poetry read it. Read it and need it. Poetry's never just entertainment like a Jacqueline Susann . . . . The poetry audience is always a fit audience, though few. It's self-selected, it reads poetry and attends poetry performances, because poetry is nourishment for the soul, for the life. And there seems to be more of it than ever.

There does, in fact, seem to be a great deal of it. If you could, would you change your part in the life you've lived in poetry so far in any way?

(Laughter) I'd be thirty-five. I've decided that if and when we get to heaven we get to pick what age we want to be. If we can't pick and choose, it isn't heaven! If I get to heaven, I get to be thirty-five as long as I want to, and probably make the same mistakes all over again. But maybe not. Maybe I'd be smarter or braver (laughter). What else? I wouldn't be a man. I would wish I could be a visual artist, like Blake. But I'd still want to be a poet.

The Mastectomy Poems

I. The Bridge

You never think it will happen to you,
What happens every day to other women.
Then as you sit paging a magazine,
It's beauties lying idly in your lap,
Waiting to be routinely waved good-bye
Until next year, the mammogram technician
Says *Sorry, we need to do this again.*

And you have already become a statistic,
Citizen of a country where the air,
Water, you estrogen, have just saluted
Their target cells, planted their Judas kiss
Inside the Jerusalem of the breast.
*Here on the film, what looks like specks of dust
Is calcium deposits.*
Go put your clothes on in a shabby booth
Whose curtain reaches halfway to the floor.
Try saying *fear.* Now feel
Your tongue as it cleaves to the roof of your mouth.

Technicalities over, medical articles read,
Decisions made, the Buick's wheels
Nose across Jersey toward the hospital
As if on monorail. Elizabeth
Exhales her poisons, Newark Airport spreads
Her wings—the planes take off over the marsh—
A husband's hand plays with a ring.

Some snowflakes whip across the lanes of cars
Slowed for the tollbooth, and two smoky gulls
Veer by the steel parabolas.
Given a choice of tunnel or bridge
Into Manhattan, the granite crust
On its black platter of rivers, we prefer
Elevation to depth, vista to crawling.

2. The Gurney

What is this long corridor above the street
What are these glazed beige tiles
Why in my horizontal state
Am I so like an undemanding child

After they wheel me in my bassinet
Into the operating room
Who made the muslin sheets so dry and white
Over my humid body's doom

How radiant the ceiling lights, of course
They buzz appealingly for me alone
I'm special, special, to my Haitian nurse
And now my surgeon pulls rubber gloves on

And now the anesthesiologist
Tells something reassuring to my ear—
And a red moon is stripping to her waist—
How good it is, not to be anywhere.

4. Mastectomy

for Alison Estabrook

I shook your hand before I went.
Your nod was brief, your manner confident,
A ship's captain, and there I lay, a chart
Of the bay, no reefs, no shoals.
While I admired your boyish freckles,
Your soft green cotton gown with the oval neck,
The drug sent me away, like the unemployed.
I swam and supped with the fish, while you
Cut carefully in, I mean
I assume you were careful.
They say it took an hour or so.

I liked your freckled face, your honesty
That first visit, when I said
What's my odds on this biopsy
And you didn't mince words,
One out of four it's cancer.
The degree on your wall shrugged slightly.
Your cold window onto Amsterdam
Had seen everything, bums and operas.
A breast surgeon minces something other
Than language.
That's why I picked you to cut me.

Was I succulent? Was I juicy?
Flesh is grass, yet I dreamed you displayed me
In pleated paper like a candied fruit,
I thought you sliced me like green honeydew
Or like a pomegranate full of seeds
Tart as Persephone's, those electric dots
That kept that girl in hell,
Those jelly pips that made her queen of death.
Doctor, you knifed, chopped, and divided it
Like a watermelon's ruby flesh
Flushed a little, serious
About your line of work
Scooped up the risk in the ducts
Scooped up the ducts
Dug out the blubber,
Spooned it off and away, nipple and all.
Eliminated the odds, nipped out
Those almost insignificant cells that might
Or might not have lain dormant forever.

5. What Was Lost

What fed my daughters, my son
Trickles of bliss,
My right guess, my true information,
What my husband sucked on
For decades, so that I thought
Myself safe, I thought love
Protected the breast.
What I admired myself, liking
To leave it naked, what I could
Soap and fondle in its bath, what tasted
The drunken airs of summer like a bear
Pawing a hive, half up a sycamore.
I'd let the sun eyeball it, surf and lake water
Reel wildly around it, the perfect fit,
The burst of praise. Lifting my chin
I'd stretch my arms to point it at people,
Show it off when I danced. I believed this pride
Would protect it, it was a kind of joke
Between me and my husband
When he licked off some colostrum
Even a drop or two of bitter milk
He'd say *You're saving for your grandchildren.*

I was doing that, and I was saving
The goodness of it for some crucial need,
The way a woman
Undoes her dress to feed
A stranger, at the end of *The Grapes of Wrath,*
A book my mother read me when I was
Spotty with measles, years before

The breast was born, but I remembered it.

How funny I thought goodness would protect it.

Jug of star fluid, breakable cup—

Someone shoveled your good and bad crumbs

Together into a plastic container

Like wet sand at the beach,

For breast tissue is like silicon.

And I imagined inland orange groves,

Each tree standing afire with solid citrus

Lanterns against the gleaming green,

Ready to be harvested and eaten.

6. December 31

I say this year no different
From any other, so we party, the poets
And physicists arrive bearing
Cheeses, chile, sesame noodles,
meats, mints, whatever—
Champagne—
Filling up the sideboard,
Filling the house up, filling it.
At midnight everyone kisses,
My man replenishes
His wicked punch,
My mother folk dances,
In the kitchen they pass a joint,
Then after that they put
The hard rock on,
And I, dressed
In black tights and a borrowed
Black and red China silk jacket,
Am that rolling stone, that
Natural woman.

No different, no
Different, and by 3 A.M. if
The son of my blood
And the wild student of my affection
Should choose to carry on, if
My goddess daughter with her satiric
Stringbean boyfriend
Tuck themselves into the bunk
Bed of her girlhood, may they hear me
Mutter in sleep, sleep
Well and happy
New year.

7. Wintering

i had expected more than this.
i had not expected to be
an ordinary woman.

Lucille Clifton

It snows and stops, now it is January,
The houseplants need feeding,
The guests have gone. Today I'm half a boy,
Flat as something innocent, a clean
Plate, just needing a story.
A woman should be able to say
I've become an Amazon,
Warrior Woman minus a breast,
The better to shook arrow
after fierce arrow.
Or else *I am that dancing Shiva*
Carved in the living rock at Elephanta,
One-breasted male deity, but I don't feel
Holy enough or mythic enough.
Taking courage, I told a man *I've resolved*
To be as sexy with one breast
As other people are with two
And he looked away.

Spare me your pity,
Your terror, your condolence.
I'm not your wasting heroine,
Your dying swan. Friend, tragedy
Is a sort of surrender.
Tell me again I'm a model
Of toughness. I eat that up.
I grade papers, I listen to the wind,
My husband helps me come, it thaws
A week before semester starts.

Now Schubert plays, and the tenor wheels
Through Heine's lieder. A fifteen-year survivor
Phones: *You know what? You're the same person
After a mastectomy as before. An idea*

That had never occurred to me.
*You have a job you like? You have poems to write?
Your marriage is okay? It will stay that way.
The wrinkles are worse. I hate looking in the mirror.
But a missing breast, well, you get used to it.*

9. Healing

Brilliant—
A day that is less than zero
Icicles fat as legs of deer
Hang in a row from the porch roof
A hand without a mitten
Grabs and breaks one off
A brandished javelin
Made of sheer
Stolen light
To which the palm sticks
As the shock of cold
Instantly shoots through the arm
To the heart—
I need a language like that,
A recognizable enemy, a clarity—
I do my exercises faithfully,
My other arm lifts,
I apply vitamin E,
White udder cream
To the howl
I make vow after vow.

11. The River

Sluiced with the city's detritus
To the glum hands of the sea,
Afraid of dark, afraid of cold,
She turns and calls for me.
When other fragments,
Each a portion gone
Before whoever loved it,
Paddling along beside her
Offer to be friends,
She shies like a spooked horse,
Shivering, whimpering—it's
As if a girl went off
From the safe playground
For a private walk and found
Herself in the wrong neighborhood
—Strange cars, strange businesses,
Too many ugly grown-ups
And none her mom. She knows
There can be no real danger
Yet it is dark, it's cold,
The ebb tide flows so swiftly,
The searching kisses of fish,
The ironic salute of crabs,
The ghostly pallid weeds
Never comfort a person.
Isn't she too big to cry?
Of course, to cry is dumb,
To be brave is smart,
Yet her lip trembles,
Carry me, mama. Sweetheart,
I hear you, I will come.

Karen Swenson

On the Edge of Things

Karen Swenson began publishing poetry in the mid-1960's, an event that now seems to mark some of the most important territory of an adult life in which she has been, often simultaneously, professor, traveler, wife, and later single mother, and poet. Born on July 29, 1936 she is the only child of Howard Swenson and Dorothy Trautman. Her childhood and adolescence were spent in a middle-class home where her father, who had no formal education beyond technical school at Pratt Institute, was an architect. Her mother, a homemaker who had attended college, came from a family that had made a good deal of money late in the last century in a Fargo, North Dakota furniture store. Before her marriage, Swenson's mother was an active, enthusiastic traveller. This love of journeys continued after her marriage and Swenson remembers, as a little girl, long drives on which her mother traversed the American countryside, reciting poetry to her daughter.

Because her parents believed that the city of New York was no place in which to raise a child, the couple moved with their daughter to Chappaqua, N.Y., an area that Swenson would later describe as "becoming a suburb," but which during her girlhood was still largely rural in character. From her childhood, Swenson recalls readily and enthusiastically, her mother's love of poetry and the fact that she allowed, and encouraged, her daughter to read widely. She remembers, as well, her confusion, in the second grade, at putting "the remains of my ice cream sandwich in the elegant, green, imitation leather pen case of a boy I adored." Less happily, but no less poignantly, she remembers that her mother was a batterer and her father an alcoholic. A favorite aunt, along with her mother, encouraged Swenson's love of literature and, perhaps while her niece was living with her in Mexico, that aunt imbued her with a deathless love of travel, a trait both of them shared with Swenson's mother. Swenson graduated from Horace Greeley High School in Chappaqua, NY, and subsequently attended Barnard College and NYU. Her thirteen-year marriage to Michael Shuter ended in divorce in the early 1960's. Her only child is a son, Michael Shuter III.

As an adult, Swenson's own feelings about what constituted a good place to live and raise children led her back to the city which her parents had fled, and for thirty-four years she maintained a home in Brooklyn while she raised her son and pursued her own frequently mobile career. Of those years, she remarks that crucial circumstances in her literary development include "being told by a number of boyfriends that I'd never be able to write good poems" and being told by her ex-husband "to stop listening to the negative things people told me about myself, my writing." It was during this period that she made the conscious decision to live — and earn her living — as a poet, a decision that led her to teaching posts and workshops in widely scattered portions of the United States.

Swenson has worked as a Professor of English Literature, conducted poetry workshops in a variety of settings including the Aspen Writers' Conference and the Rhode Island University Writers' Conference, and been Poet-in-Residence at Skidmore College, the University of Idaho, and Denver University, among others. She has also worked as a poet-in-residence in Nebraska, Colorado, Montana, New Hampshire, Virginia, Connecticut, Idaho, and Pennsylvania through the Poets in the Schools Program. For the past ten years, in the spirit of the love of travel that has been hers almost as long as she can remember, she has spent at least two months of every twelve in Asia, traveling in Hong Kong, Taipei, China, Vietnam, Thailand, Cambodia, Laos, Burma, Indonesia, Bhutan, and most recently Tibet.

Today, she takes refuge from the demands of work in cooking, listening to opera, and the company of her cat. She is beginning work on a travel book about her most recent trip to Asia, which included a dusty "twenty-six days in the back of a baby blue Chinese truck." Her four books of poems are *An Attic of Ideals* (Doubleday, 1974), the chapbook *East-West* (Confluence, 1980), *A Sense of Direction* (The Smith, 1989) and the 1993 National Poetry Series winner *The Landlady in Bangkok* (Copper Canyon, 1994). Swenson's poetic voice is at once compassionate and clinically precise, her consciousness discerning and receptive to whatever the world offers.

In one of your earlier poems, "The Psychologist," you describe a woman arranging her brows "to the level of the day." That struck me, when I read it, as a quintessentially Swenson line (laughter) — that levelness is extremely important in your work from the "The Psychologist" *through* Sense of Direction *to* The Landlady in Bangkok *and beyond.*

Yes, well, that's interesting. I don't think I ever quite recognized that in myself.

But does it make sense to you?

Yes. Oh yes! It does. Balance. When I was still drinking, one night as I was getting sloshed, and increasingly self-critical, I wrote down on a piece of paper that I lacked balance and perspective and proportion.

Indeed! You always seem to be balancing elements — image & emotion, self and other, poet and subject — while maintaining a rooted, level stance. No small feat. Just for instance, you seem to balance age and experience with searing images in The Landlady in Bangkok. *How does the book's epigraph, "Old women ought to be explorers," resonate with your own experience as a woman and a poet?*

Tyros reinvent the wheel. You need to know before you are ready to explore. The best exploration is based on a foundation of knowledge/experience. That's true of both intellectual and physical exploration.

It took me many years of writing in free verse to become ready to investigate form, meter, rhyme. It took me many years of writing confessionally before I ventured out beyond self and family. My life experiences moved me along that trajectory — having a child, having a divorce (both birth experiences) and being an itinerant poet. In youth, it is so important to belong, to be part of. Later one can become interested in apart from, in being alien. Although I felt more alien as a young woman than I do now.

Being a woman is for me being an alien in the world. Most cultures are organized so that if you are a woman, you are on the outside looking in.

Certainly you were an alien in Asia, both ethnically and culturally. What is it like to be the alien in those contexts?

I find it's very freeing. In one's own society one is always imprisoned in the culture's rules. To be alien is to be outside the rules. That, of course, isn't really true, since actually you become subject to a new set of rules and to make it trickier, you usually don't know what those rules are. In 1974 I went to Iran taking my twelve-year-old son along as protection — it's one thing to travel alone as "woman" and something quite different to travel as a "mother," particularly in a Moslem country — and found the men were so astonished by my lonely presence on buses and in tea houses they decided to treat me like a man. This was occasionally inconvenient but certainly better than being treated like a Moslem woman. Being alien magnificently wrenches me out of my culture, gives me a chance to view what we take for granted as much as breathing, to see those cultural constructions that imprison as well as those that I am interested in, from a different perspective. I get to test its [the culture's] values, see if I agree. There are many Western or American cultural beliefs that I find anywhere from repulsive to silly. The Thais, for instance, make very little fuss about sexual preference. You should produce children. After that, it's your problem. It is so much more sensible than our hysterical insistence on heterosexuality.

An advantage for women who travel alone is the exhilaration of sloughing off, like snake skin, our "at home" roles — daughter, wife, mother — which leaves us a little naked and very much a mystery to ourselves and others. Another advantage is that we, more than men, are responsible for our surroundings. We often do home maintenance for a living, so what delight to be in a hotel room where we are responsible for nothing — bed, sink or husband's breakfast.

Although you claim "old womanhood" as a position from which to write, the writer you are today must have origins further back in time. Was there something in your background, your childhood, that created the poet?

My mother read poetry to me when I was a child, not just nursery rhymes, but Frost and Masefield. She also, on long drives — my childhood was full of long drives — whether they were Westchester to Manhattan or Westchester to North Dakota) would recite huge hunks of "Hiawatha" thumping the rhythm out with her palm on the steering wheel. She thought it was a howl, and would declaim in ranting style. Everyone but the cat and dog in our house went to bed with a book, and when I was fifteen and living with my aunt Liz in Mexico I was allowed, oh joy, to read at the dining room table.

My mother had a real feeling for words. She enjoyed the sound of them in her mouth, the possibilities of them and loved putting them together so that they startled.

If pain makes poets I had my portion. My mother was a batterer and my father was an active alcoholic, as I was for many years.

What I saw — the description of what I saw — clearly became important to me. I grew up believing in the importance of communication — that relationships, events, could be altered through communication.

Given that your mother was a batterer, can you discuss "The White Rabbit" in light of that information? What made you, after many years, recreate in a poem what must have been a traumatic experience?

What happened was that my mother died. And I think everybody's got this kind of experience in life — that there are certain stories one doesn't tell until the person is dead. My ex-husband has been gravely ill — and I wonder about the implications of that because I've blanked large pieces of my marriage. I can't — I just can't remember! All I remember is that I was unhappy. I can't remember anything specific. But once my mother died, that incident of killing the rabbit came. . .it had always been there, I hadn't forgotten it. . .but it had always been covered and suddenly it came to the fore and it became something that I felt I had to write about. If it wasn't successful I would put it back in the drawer. And I felt that in writing about it I had to be absolutely truthful about what I had done. That this was not an attempt to blame the parent without taking responsibility for what I had done. There's a joke about some guys on a ship, and the captain yells at the first mate and the first mate yells at the sailor and the sailor yells at the parrot. This was the same sort of sequence. I was just taking it out on what couldn't hurt me. I wanted that clear, and — sometimes I want fixed endings — but this time I didn't want a fixed ending. I wanted that truth that is the kind that sends you back to try to figure out what happened to you, that's caused who you are now. It's an incident like this that you can gather your forces around and start archeology.

Personal archeology?

Personal archeology. (laughter)

That's a pretty good description of a lot of poetry. There's a poem in your most recent work — "Without Reservations"— that seems to have that "archeological" quality. Did this poem, also, arise from your mother's death?

No. This death was my Aunt Elizabeth's. She lived to be within two weeks of her hundredth birthday, and I adored her! I think I adored her largely because I needed to adore. My mother had taken herself out of the game by being a batterer. And I credited Liz with many of the things that I now realize belonged to my mother.

Was this the aunt who let you read at the table?

Yes. And this was the aunt I went to Mexico with. She was the one who provided me with my first trip abroad at the age of fourteen or fifteen, when I lived with her in Mexico.

So there is a considerable debt there?

Oh! There's a big debt. She was able to do things that a parent has difficulty doing because the parent is too nervous. I was allowed to read by my mother, I have to say, just about anything I wanted. Only boy (!) did my mother get nervous about sex. Liz got nervous about sex too, but she coped by ignoring it. (Laughter)

That's actually helpful sometimes.

It was! It's more helpful to a kid! Liz also gave very interesting explanations. I'm not sure that they were necessarily true, but they were interesting explanations. I was fifteen, and I knew enough about Hemingway to know that he was not someone who was given to religion. I suspect that in my family he had something of a reputation as a Commie. I had read *For Whom the Bell Tolls*, and in reading it I was very impressed. But at the end when they go out to face the opposition, one of the men in the troop starts to say the "Our Father" or the "Hail Mary"—I can't remember which at a distance of so many years—and I said to Liz, "But Hemingway doesn't believe in this. So why did he put this in the book?" And her answer was "Because he's a good writer and he knows about people." I thought—and still think—that was an A+ answer.

She was, I would say, one very smart reader!

She was a very smart woman, but she refused to accept the title of intellectual. When I would say to her, "You know, Liz, you're really an intellectual," she would respond with "Oh no, dear!" But she was. She spent her time thinking. I guess, particularly once she got into her nineties. She didn't tell me how much things were falling apart—I guess people don't. It's too humiliating. I would say that she spent the years from 92 to her death — she wasn't able to read any more because she forgot between the first part of a sentence and the period what was going on— thinking about things. So she gave away all her books and she sat there and thought. She thought a lot about her own past. Her mother had been a real stinker, a real brimstone bitch. The problem was simply that she should have run General Motors. She had enormous ambition. She chose a sort of wobbly husband whom she then tried to drive. Of course that didn't work. She took it out on her kids because she was so furious. And Liz—she was the oldest, my mother was twelve years younger—Liz had received most of the pummeling from this woman. She spent the last seven years of her life trying to work that out.

Do you think she did?

She certainly worked some things out. I'm always amazed. She was a Catholic woman, very much of the old school. One day she told me that she had joined the Eastern Star. Catholic women of her generation wouldn't go near that. But her father had been a member. It was a way of getting closer to him. She missed him. So there were things that she did, trying to work it out. She said to me one time when I came into town "You know, I think my mother's relatives really made her life Hell, when her marriage went sour. They marked her. They made her feel she was a failure. I think that's one of the reasons she was so rotten." I got a certain amount of it too, ill treatment from my grandmother, and grandparents don't usually do that.

When did you come to realize that you actually were a battered child? That this was not the universal human condition.

Ahh — in my thirties. As children we tend to think that our lives are simply the way things are.

And in the midst of what now looks like a rather chaotic childhood and adolescence, when did you know — and how did you know — that you were a poet?

I had rigid ideas about what constituted a poet and would not say I was a poet, although I would say I wrote, until I was published. Thinking that way caused me trouble. Early in my career, I went for long periods between getting published. That set me up for believing I was no longer a poet, as well as for feelings of failure.

I did not come from people who thought you could become a poet by deciding to be one, or even by doing the work involved. You had to have confirmation from the outside. To my parents, you were what the world *told* you you were. This caused them and me much unhappiness.

What has kept you writing poems all these years?

It certainly wasn't encouragement. I suspect I actually like to write, although I have managed to hide this fact from myself for many years. My Germanic background dictates that you should not like what you do, anything else would be despicable self indulgence. I also kept going because the task itself is so enthrallingly complex.

In terms of poetry and meaning, what is it that you do when you write poems?

A poem often starts as an unattached image — like the betel box in "The Cambodian Box." As I write I reveal to myself why that image is important to me. For me, the basis of all art is communication. An electrician is an expert on the wiring in my house. I am his expert at the communication of emotion and meaning. The artist has always been the fountainhead of significance in any culture. An artist attempts to express an understanding of life within the given cultural guidelines and if the guidelines are inadequate in some way, you break through them. Emily Dickinson certainly did that.

I'm not sure when or why meaning began to leak out of Western culture. Perhaps it was the loss of God, or the Industrial Revolution and the separation from the land, but accompanying that drain has been the loss of ordinary people's interest in art. Art has become a specialty, like ophthalmic surgery, too complex, too abstruse for the average reader or viewer. This in turn has caused art to move away from people and towards institutions. Poetry became a school lesson, not fun, or beauty or excitement. Painting began to appear in corporate headquarters. Devoid of meaning, a painting will offend no one, will merely show how cultured, well meaning or rich Exxon is. Exxon is not going to hang Munch's "The Scream" in corporate headquarters.

I feel, as is apparent in "We," that my responsibility is to investigate the significance of things. I don't mean that I am looking for a moral, but I am looking for the connection between people, between the world and us. I feel the best writers do this —Linda Hogan, for instance. Doing that increases the risks I take, since the reader may not agree with my meaning, or like it. I can be wrong. Trying to elucidate significance may make me sentimental or spiteful or judgmental. There are a lot of things to trip over once you get involved with meaning. I want a poem to be beautiful, but I also want it to be involved in the world of ideas— thought and emotions.

So how does a poem — let's take "The Cambodian Box" as an example — get itself onto the page? What is the experience of writing the poem as you live it?

I bought a silver betel box in Bangkok in the form of a pair of geese nestled in a basket. I recognized the work as Cambodian. It

was an exquisite little sculpture—each feather distinctly etched
and the lovely roundness of the geese. I began to track it back-
wards, to think about how and why it had come into my posses-
sion. A woman or man had tucked it, perhaps with others, into a
sarong or bag and run from the Khmer Rouge, Pol Pot.

The West's tendency to see good and evil as separate entities
rather than as connected paradoxes has always seemed to me one
of the great weaknesses of our philosophical and religious think-
ing. It is, to me, quite apparently untrue. I find the East attractive
because there opposites are integral to each other. The little betel
box seemed to me to be an example of this paradox of human
skill in creation and destruction, of beauty and torture. These are
the opposing kinds of craftsmanship of which we are capable.

Your book before last, **A Sense of Direction,** *contains poem after
poem that is deeply personal. Was your subject when that book
was written different from your subject today?*

I doubt that I have that kind of overview of my work. I would
guess, however, that the details have changed from personal to
cultural while the obsessions have stayed the same. Certainly the
role of women is an obsession in my first book (*An Attic of
Ideals*), *A Sense of Direction*, and in *Landlady*. The importance of
accepting responsibility for one's actions is as present in "The
White Rabbit" as in "We."

*Let's go back to Liz's "A+ response" to Hemingway—"a good writer
and he knows about people." Take "What's Broken," one of the new
poems from your most recent trip to Tibet. The poem seems to cap-
ture a new tone—religious, or spiritual perhaps—in your work.*

You know, I think it is. It's an attempt to find some kind of reso-
lution, I think as Liz was trying. I think it's exactly what Liz was
doing. I think it has to do with being the age I am now.

*But isn't it also "being a good writer and knowing about
people"—not so much in the sense of knowing audience as know-
ing the way people's lives work out?*

Right. And I do feel, as I've said before, that I'm just very average, in a sense. Whatever I'm writing about is what one writes about at this stage of life. I'd like to go back to that "old woman" epigraph. I said that there was movement from writing about family to writing about Asia. A young woman came up to me at the end of (I think) a classroom session, and she said, very carefully, "*I don't know whether this is true, Ms. Swenson, but I feel that there was a growing up that happened between writing about your family and writing about the outside world.*" And yes, I think there is. I think she was right. I think you say, *Okay. I'm done with this. It was important and had to be done, but now I'm done with it and it's time to move on.* It's an important thing to do — to turn outward.

You almost suggest that there's a movement from self, to the family, to the larger world, and then back into the self.

Well, the self goes with you, so there isn't much you can do about it.

I was thinking specifically about your Aunt Liz and her enforced turn inward in old age, into what I suppose was the center of the self, while the world was falling away.

Yet if she hadn't lost the ability to read, I don't know that she would have done that with her life. This was someone who was fascinated by history and who was also a traveler. But, well, yes.

Now let's go back in time. At one point in your career, when a budget crunch left you jobless, you made a clear decision to live by poetry, becoming what you have called "an itinerant poet"— what did that choice cost you, and what did it give you?

It cost me a Ph.D. in Old English and made my son, I fear, feel abandoned, but it gained me a new sense of self and an intimate knowledge of parts of my country I would not otherwise have seen. Traveling is for me, always, a spiritual journey. I spent six years driving in the Rockies, where it always seemed to be February. I was told in a southern Colorado town where I was doing PITS (Poets in the Schools) work, *We don't have trouble with Anglos here. We don't have any Anglos here.* It was the beginnings of my travel, the start of my confrontation with my fears.

My journeys also gave me glimpses of other people's lives that shook me out of the "quiet tenor" of my ways. In that same southern Colorado town I taught a young man, the most talented high school student I had ever been lucky enough to encounter. I noticed that he had three deep scars on his cheek. I couldn't imagine what they were from. I asked his teacher, who told me without any sense that there was anything odd in what she said, *In seventh grade he decided he was an atheist, and therefore he had to be scarred. He makes the wounds with his razor and keeps them open.*

As poet and teacher, how did you perceive those scars at the time?

With horror at the lack of understanding on the part of the community that surrounded him. I tried to see that he would get into college. He refused to take the SAT. When I returned to that town, he wouldn't come to school while I was in the town. The whole incident broke my heart, that such talent should behave so punitively toward itself; but that is what an industrial culture frequently does to art.

**In Landlady *you quote Eric Fromm, "Evilness is a specifically* human phenomenon." *Why did you choose that particular sentence?*

Evil has always been with us. In the West we have seen it from various angles over the centuries, as sin, as psychosis — we have moved from thinking of it as something willed to something uncontrolled. That, I think, is progress. It is specifically human because evil requires consciousness. A cat is cruel to a mouse by our standards but the cat has no consciousness, therefore, no empathy, and therefore, cruel doesn't exist for a cat. Knowledge of good and evil presupposes an ability to imagine oneself as both victim and victimizer. When governments want to make their people into conscienceless killers, the first thing they do is to dehumanize the enemy and make people afraid. What you dehumanize and what you fear you remove from the arena of empathy. Words help: *Gook, Kike.* When you live in terror of being killed it is much easier to kill.

In the individual torturer or sex criminal, as in your ordinary person, the lineage is from victim to victim. Alice Miller has worked this out magnificently in her books. If you have been victimized you will victimize. The eleven-year-old who killed the fourteen-year-old who was in turn killed by his gang had cigarette burns all over his body because he had been tortured as a child. You cannot expect children to be either nice children or nice adults if you burn them with cigarettes. Evil is just an old hand-me-down from father to son, from mother to daughter.

It's pretty obvious that you have a genuine lust for travel—in part a legacy from Liz and your mother, and that even extremely painful episodes associated with travel have done nothing to assuage it.

Yeah. I just get happy. And I get happy talking about it. Walking into a Thai restaurant I smell that smell and I'm happy.

Part of what this lust for travel has given you is The Landlady in Bangkok, *which was the "big" one—the National Poetry Series winner. As long as we're talking about movement, what effect has that prize had on the movement of your career?*

Well, I don't know that it's movement. I don't know what kind of change it's made. One immediate difference is that now people know who I am. For years I had been assiduous at trying to get readings and do that sort of thing. The prize gave me a real boost. I found that people were much more interested in having me read. I think what prizes do—for the people who run English departments and reading series, and that sort of thing—is help them differentiate. I'm not saying that they're bad because they use prizes that way. It just seems to me that there's such a mass of material out there that it's very hard for anyone to deal with.

Given that mass of work, much of it very fine, do you see a downside to literary prizes? Do you want to comment on the imminent demise of arts funding in this country?

Oh, well, I think that's terrible. That is just American barbarianism and very typical of us in that we really funded the arts because the Russians funded the arts. We were ashamed at how miserly we were during the Cold War. We had to measure up, and so we put money into the arts. Now, unfortunately, our rivals are going to be the Chinese, who go around tramping on the arts.

Who had the Cultural Revolution?

Yes. That's right. And destroyed. So we've got nobody pushing us and we need to be pushed. We are not a country that is lavish in this area. The French are always lavish, the Italians, I guess, are semi-lavish, and the English, you know, they couldn't possibly let the French get ahead of them, so they're in there. Of course, the Scandinavian peninsula people are really involved. And I have no idea what poor Russia is up to at the moment — just trying to hang in there and stay alive, I suspect. We really are a peasant culture.

Whether giving prizes is a good thing, I think, it depends on the receiver's psychological state, because 90% of the time, probably, perhaps more often, it's wonderful. But recently I realized that when I was — maybe sixteen or seventeen — with a totally low sense of self-esteem and parents who thought that if you praised the child all hell would break loose immediately and you would have a juvenile delinquent immediately (laughter) —

And look what they got!

(more laughter) A juvenile delinquent. Anyway, I was writing in an after school creative writing class. I wrote something the teacher really liked, and she said "Why don't we send this to Literary Cavalcade," which was the Scholastic magazine. "They're having a prize. Why don't we send it?" I was just thrilled — that's what was important to me — that she thought it was that important. It had a devastating effect on me. It made me so perfectionistic that I couldn't write stories anymore. I thought I had to be some sort of super human being. The result was that I would think of a plot and think "Oh no! It's been done!" as if every plot in the world hasn't been done—as though that had anything to do with it. Of course I couldn't voice this to anyone because I was so dreadfully ashamed. The result was that I switched from short story writing to poetry. That's really how I became a poet.

So you did make the switch from prose to verse. Has that been a good thing on the whole?

I think so.

Why?

I think that's probably where I belong, because I'm more of a jeweler than your fiction writer is, and poets are, generally speaking, jewelers. They take the words and they set them. They put them into settings so that they shine from as many facets as possible.

Do you think the poet's sensibility is in any way inherently different from the prose writer's? Not so much in the setting, perhaps, as in what the poet sees from which to draw the jewels?

I'm not sure. I think the big difference between prose and poetry has to do with how you view the use of words. Sy Epstein, who taught at Denver, whom I stole that metaphor about the jeweler from, says that when he was young he would read poetry and think *Why would anybody want to do that with words?* I think *What else would you want to do? Why would you want to treat them as though they were just ordinary building blocks instead of these extraordinary multifaceted gems?*

The sophisticate's Legos?

Right. Literary Legos.

What are you planning next in terms of writing?

I'm trying to write about the experiences I've had in Tibet. I'm having a hard time for some reason or other. I think it's more difficult because it's more spiritual.

There we come back to that shift in tone that I noticed. . .

Yes. Spiritual. That is the shift in tone. It seems to me that *The Landlady in Bangkok*—and I can imagine other people saying

What are you talking about?—that it's a political book in many, many ways. Its concerns are frequently political. How women are treated, how people are treated. It's a very secular book, but it seems to me that it goes at things from a political angle. That will exist in the next book, no doubt about it, but I am at least semi-consciously aware that I'm trying to write less about Tibet exclusively, that I am trying to write poems that are sort of 50-50 West and Tibet—"Offering" being one, where the western religion is there with the eastern religion. It's one of the poems that I'm really happy with.

When did you start writing "Offering?" Do you remember a moment? An image?

A sensory experience of being in—one after the other—Buddhist shrines in Tibet, smelling the dairy odor that comes from butter lamps, feeling that there are odors that are forever associated with events, experiences—not that I'm going to smell this anywhere else. That's crazy. You're going to go to Trenton, you think, and you're going to meet a yak butter lamp on somebody's dresser (laughter)—but in northern Thailand, for instance, there's an odor that I identify with that experience and trekking those hills. It's the odor of woodsmoke in the tiny villages. It's the same thing—that darkness, the dairy odor (which I like, though some people can't bear it). There's something about it like home in a funny kind of way. I grew up in what was becoming a suburb, and I went to dairy farms. That's a nice smell—that milky nourishing smell. You have that as well as the flickering of the lamps and the awesomeness of people who just believe. They just—believe. And it is the core of their lives.

What does that actually mean to someone (albeit with a high tolerance for butter lamps) from a vastly different, western culture?

Oh, but it's not, you know. It's not as different as you might think. There were two guys, I think they were Capuchins—I don't think they were Franciscans, but I can look it up — one of whose names was H-u-c, French, and in the sixteenth century they went drifting across Tibet with the idea that they were doing a survey for the Holy See about the possibility of sending out missionaries and converting people. They kept saying to each other *The Tibetans must have had some contact with the Catholic Church. This is so much like the Catholic church—except that it's wrong.* There is a familiarity, like the old Catholic church with its dark interiors, its flickering lamps, its infinite side aisles, apses, its incense and saints. The costumes that the priests wear. There is a superficial similarity. A great similarity.

What about the absoluteness of the faith? What does that, for instance, feel like to an outsider?

The interesting thing is that it has not been used, since about the sixteenth century, to discriminate against others. It has not been used to knock others off. There were fights in the sixteenth century, there have been struggles for power in the various orders of Buddhism in Tibet, but there's not that absolutism that the Catholic Church has about . . . oh . . .

Soul saving?

Yeah. The Inquisition. It isn't that kind—although in a way the Spanish Inquisition, on some level, has a similarity in its rigidity and in its horror with the Cultural Revolution. That massive kind of human destructiveness because of absolute belief. Tibetans are very nice about you not believing. They don't mind much. I have prayer beads that were given me by a woman in a nunnery in Lhasa, and you can't—(for reasons that I do not understand) find them anymore. You can find prayer beads, but you cannot find these prayer beads, which were carved, I suspect, by the nomads. They were carved of yak bone. At least I hope they were yak bone because if it isn't it's human. When I wear those beads, Tibetans want to know that I know what to do with them. Once they know that I know what to do with them, they leave me alone. It's up to me. I'm just another species. They don't feel that they have to get in there and run me. Buddhism, while it does get controlling occasionally, hasn't been so for many years. And that's nice.

If we treat all this as background, it really illuminates the last sentence of "Offering."

Yes it does. I don't think that would have been a possible sentence in *The Landlady in Bangkok*. I don't think it was something that was interesting to me at that time.

There seems to be much less anger—less outrage.

Oh! That would be so true. I think that's what that young woman in Illinois was saying to me. She was saying that I was moving away from that early rage, to anger at the way the way the world is, at the way it's run. All my friends in Thailand see this as a Buddhist conversion. I think to some extent they may be right. I'm just incapable of joining any religion, since I feel that all religions are male constructs that marginalize women.

When you travel, you must meet not only Asians but also Europeans and others who are fellow travellers from the west.

Yes. And I've never successfully written about that. I have a poem and it just doesn't work. That's why it isn't in *Landlady*. But I'm fascinated by that.

What makes some of your fellow travellers compelling to you?

Because on this trip particularly—26 days on a baby blue Chinese truck—we were, many of us (not all of us by any means) on that truck because we were looking for something, and trying to make up our minds about things. There was a Danish man about twelve years younger than I. It was his fifth time in Tibet, and his second time circumambulating Mt. Kailash. He's not a believer, but there's a need there. He recognizes that being alone in the landscape of Tibet is something that appeals to his spirit. He brings to it all of the, probably unfortunate, western logic and analytic training, which I suspect is a great nuisance to us as well as a great boon. There was a young Australian woman, and we would discuss Karma. It was very interesting. Other people on the trip had nothing to do with this. There was a couple from Spain who were traveling with a German friend. These people travelled as though they were going through an art gallery. This is a pretty village, that is a pretty mountain. They wanted no contact — no real contact except in a manner of service from the local population. I don't think they were even aware of it, but they were sort of afraid of that contact. Then we had two men from the United States with whom I organized the trip. Certainly one of them, his interest had to do with challenge, doesn't care where it is — it's a mountain and he's going to climb that mountain. They had a shot at Everest and they ended up in very serious trouble. They were extremely lucky to get back. People travel in different ways. There was another German — a man named Klaus — who travels the way I hope I travel, although he's younger and stronger and possibly more daring in some ways. Klaus just gets totally involved — with the people around, and he's very good at dealing with situations where oil is needed on the waters. There are many, many different ways, and I'm fascinated by that. Why are we here? What do we think we're doing?

Your mention of Klaus suggests this question — when you travel, do you ever miss being younger?

If you mean by that having certain kinds of physical strength, yes. But that is just about all I miss. Going around Kailash, I thought "how nice it would have been to do this at forty-five instead of almost sixty." (Laughter) It wouldn't have been so difficult.

Would it have been as rewarding?

I don't think so. I don't think I would have been able to relax into the experience in the same way. It's taken me ten years of doing this kind of traveling to begin to relax into it. Still, I'm far from where I would like to be.

Which is?

Which is a woman named Jean — I have no idea what her last name is — who is sixty-two, white-haired. She appears to be built out of rawhide and she's from Luxembourg. Jean is estranged from her family who would not talk to her because she decided at a young age that she would rather travel than get married and have a family. She has traveled ever since then—everyplace in the world that you can think of. She was hitchhiking, or attempting to hitchhike, out of Tibet and back into China. She got stopped near the border. The young Chinese guard looked at her and said *My mother wouldn't do this.* Then he said *I have to turn you back. I have no option on that. I have to turn you back. But I will not fine you.* The fine was a whopping fine—I think it was $500.00. So Jean came back to Lhasa on somebody's truck. But Jean does that. She just travels around hitchhiking. She has—and she admits to this—no fear. Now that is an enormous advantage, because you present yourself to people totally differently, in a limpid, transparent manner, when you have no fear. It causes people, therefore, to react differently to you. It makes all the difference.

It would. Yet transparency is such a curious aspect of personal presentation, one we see so seldom.

That's right. Particularly in the Western world. I think that we're suspicious of it because it is so rare. But it can only be done when you are comfortable with who you are and what you are and what you've done in the world, when you are not sitting there tensed for the judgment that you're sure is coming at you.

Are you suggesting that you, yourself, are tensed "for the judgment?"

Very frequently. But I'm getting better.

And that you're not utterly content—with who you are or what you've done?

I don't know that I'm capable of that. I may be. There may be a point where you let go. I suspect there is. But it's a wonderful thing. Being around Jean was just delightful. And fascinating. She has all kinds of very interesting ideas.

Is there a difference between being an explorer and being a traveller?

Yeah. I think the built-in thing is that if you're an explorer you're going where no one of your particular race, at any rate, has gone.

". . . to boldly go . . .?"

(Laughter) That's right! Where no woman has gone before. Whereas to be a traveller is to be, perhaps, on the edge of things. But not to be that first one.

And Jean?

Is a traveller.

What judgment are you tensed for?

(Laughter) Do you charge $80.00 an hour?

Would that I could!

Well, I think that what I'm tensed for are the judgments that were made long ago, and that we learn by the age of five are going to come at us and that we think, then, forever are going to come at us.

And will define us?

And will define us, yes. Those things are long gone actually. We almost all live in a past that's very dead—whose carcass is, indeed, rotting away around us if the bones aren't long since picked clean. But that we have great difficulty accepting that this is true, because we've incorporated the parents into the head.

Still—we always seem to be faced with judgments. As writers, for instance, we face reviews—and let's face it, there are reviews, and then there are reviews.

There are. But consider. If Keats hadn't been quite so young and quite so desperate, he wouldn't have taken those reviews quite so hard—those were real bitch reviews. They were really mean-spirited reviews. Those just happen. I think one of the things you learn as you go along is that that sort of review has to do with the other person. It very rarely has to do with you. So you have to give it up. To harbor that, to worry about it, is just foolishness. The curious thing is that you recognize those reviews when you see them about other people. After all, the point of reviews is to help the public. That's what they're about, so that you make up your mind whether to read that book. Some reviews, like one I saw in *The Times* recently, are simply dismissive, so that I wondered why they even ran the damned thing. The review never told the reader enough — you couldn't form any idea whether to read the book or not.

There's another danger — of sorts. Very often, in the wrong hands, a book will hit a nerve — like that story I told you about the woman who came up to me after a reading and proceeded to confuse my father with her father, to conflate them, and to tell me all about a poem I had written about my father. She scared the bejesus out of me. She had no barriers between herself and me. I found that frightening; I find it frightening when poems hit people that way. I suppose there's a certain inevitability about it. Perhaps I should be grateful when my work hits the nerves that way, that I'm doing something, but I'd rather not be in its presence.

Tell me, in a life as rich with travel and the love of travel as yours, why have you for years maintained a home in Brooklyn? Has the sale of that house been a release or grief?

Well, I was in that house for thirty-four years. I am, apparently, still learning the importance to me of a base. When I sold the house, I began to fall apart sort of — and it has continued. I am very brittle. By now most of my friends know that I take things much more personally than usual. I have great difficulty just letting stuff go by. You need friends at this stage. I am in limbo as far as housing goes, and here I am affronting people. That isn't a big help. So I apparently really need a base. That would make sense. I mean, who travels best but she who has a base?

And Jean?

Well, she has a base, in Luxembourg, and I wouldn't be at all surprised to find out that it's very important to her. It probably isn't, any more, being filled up with things. Travelling, you go through a phase of collecting things, but then you stop. On the other hand, I was dying to go through Jean's backpack and find out what she was travelling with, because over the years I have cut down enormously (not just on collecting), but she had cut down farther than I had ever dreamed of cutting back.

One thing about a base. I do, I get very fragile without one.

If you could (magically) revise the life you have lived, what would you change?

I wouldn't have stayed married as long as I did. I was married for thirteen years. But I wouldn't give away my son, of course. Because I was raised Catholic, I thought you had to keep on trying. You don't. (Chuckle) You can quit and get out. It would have been nice not to be an alcoholic, because I would have been able to utilize my life. There's twenty years of my life where I utilized what I had way under what should have been going on. And it was because of alcoholism.

Is there a connection between stopping drinking and being a poet?

Do you mean a change in the writing?

Maybe. Does one give a center to the other?

Well, I grew up in the grand days when you had to be either insane or an alcoholic in order to write. Particularly, perhaps, if you were female. We had Plath and Sexton. And the young buy into that sort of thing because it's drama, but I don't think there's any doubt that if I continued to drink I would have died, as a poet, and probably, finally, lingeringly, also as a person. There is a picture of Jean Rhys that you probably know. She is very thin, she is older, and she is standing in a doorway with a martini glass in her hand. That picture just gives me the chills. The expression on her face — I know that whole thing, and it is for me filled with terror. It is the dissolution of self. It seems to me that what happens to people a great deal of the time, if not always, whether male or female, if they drink and write, is that they end up chasing their own tails. Everything's fine up to a certain point, and then they're reproducing themselves — round and round and round — instead of growing. I think giving up the drinking allowed me to grow. I certainly wasn't growing while I was drinking.

You wouldn't say, then, that writing made it possible for you to

quit . . .

I became aware, at some point in the drinking, that it wasn't helping the writing, that it was killing the writing. From that standpoint, yes, I think it helped me to stop drinking because the writing is, for me, the reason for being alive. So what was the point, if I wasn't going to be able to write. Those last years, before I quit — I can't be certain — I have no clear idea because I didn't date my work at that time, but my guess is that there's damned little that got salvaged out of the last two — three years. That was part of why I had to stop. Because I was going to lose the thing that was most important to me in the world. And then I was going to die, slowly and horribly. My father lived to be seventy-eight, guzzling all the way.

The White Rabbit

Yes, Mother,
holding the bannister with five-year-old fingers
muffled in Sunday gloves
I did come down the stairs
in my daffodil coat from Best's
in my straw hat with the brown ribbons down my back
and the round elastic that sliced my throat.

Thirty-five years I've tried to remember
what we fought about in your upstairs bedroom
that I've wiped from the inside of my mind—
the house ends for me at the top of the stair—
although I can smell your scent
the bottle with the perched crystal doves.

Dressed in your will of clothes
I watch you pin hat to hair in the mirror
while my small voice hurls itself against you
and a fly blunders into your glass hat
falling into the powder in the pink box.

Like butter on pancakes
the sun melts on the front porch.
I unlatch the hutch
peel the white cotton from my hands
and beat the rabbit to death,
that plump passivity of flesh
soft as your talcumed thighs.

When you discovered the rabbit
your hand snaked the dog chain round my legs
each blow winding and unwinding pain
on the bobbin of my scream.
You beat the badness from your doll.
I wished you dead.

But I kept my secret even while
I carried the cigar box
to your chant of accusations.
All those words have dissolved
into the swamp gas of nightmares.

Twenty years later
you apologized in the car,
said it couldn't have been just me,
must have been all of us
picking it up by the ears—
a hemorrhage.
I listened but didn't confess.
You, eyes taut to the road,
never mentioned the whipping
and I,
now that you're dead
just as I wanted you to be
come back to climb the stairs.

The Cambodian Box

The silver betel box is formed by two geese
nestled closely as a contented couple
in their silver scallops of feathers.

Empty in the shop window in Bangkok
of all but its beauty,
what household of servants and polished teak
did it belong to
before it came through the jungle in a pocket
to buy a month's rice?

The able hands
brown as bread crusts
that formed this sheen of necks and breasts
are matched by another pair,
the color of rouge,
which practice death's craft
in the paradox of hands
mated perfectly as these shining geese.

We

In a museum of the city
once called Saigon, are snapshots. One's
been blown up so we can all see
it clearly. An American,

a young foot soldier, stands on battle
pocked land, his helmet at a jaunty
tilt, posed for buddies as the Model
Grunt. In his left hand he is dangling,

like Perseus, a head by its hair.
Though not Medusa's, it's his charm
for turning fear to stone. It's stare
will quiet, awhile, his throbbing chest.

The tattered flesh that once dressed collar
bones hangs rags from this Vietnamese
neck, captured with the soldier's scar
of a grin by a friend's camera.

Is it enough to see it clearly?
We all know what to think. The whitewashed
walls of a second room show nearly
as many black and white shots of

Cambodian atrocities
against Vietnamese. No room's hung
with what was done to enemies
of Vietnam just as there's no

American museum built
to show off snapshots of My Lai.
One pronoun keeps at bay our guilt
they they they they they they they they.

Without Reservations

Each visit we arranged her death — the list
of guests, new underclothes in tissue paper.
We sorted the inscriptions in the shoebox —
her scrawl on scraps of paper — "Bury me,
no matter what the weather, in my pink
dress, pin the chiffon scarf with my blue brooch.

That Sunday, when I asked how she was, she
snapped like a screendoor on its spring, "The way
you are at 99." I said, "Fine, but I'll
be furious with you if you die and
don't tell me." We laughed. In ten minutes she
called back, "Come. That is what is happening."
The shoebox done, in the Dakota kiln
of summer, with the fan at our feet turning
between us leisurely, we sat. She asked,
"There will be money. Where will you go when
I die?" The fan's breath flurried at my hem,
a murmur of moths. "Tibet." "Yes," she said.

The first stroke ate my name, the voices of
many words. She sat on the bed blowing
her nose on the top sheet as I arranged
for nurses. The next stroke came in September
while I taught. In October the home called
to say she had turned her face to the wall.

She would not eat or drink. "Tubes," they said. "No
tubes," I said. "Two days," they said. I looked at
her slides of Guatemala, riffled through
her guide to Luxor, booked a flight to Fargo
and knew I was an orphan. The scarf was pinned.
The guests invited. She left without reservations.

Offering

A black hat in a Sunday pew,
her silent aisle was circled by
the sea of sonorous hosannas.
Deaf to the sermon she was a blown
fuse in the spiritual circuit—
God to priest to the unordained souls.
In her, the sermon's vacancy,
its silence, was an empty bowl
open to the pouring of her
soul's voice. God answered back? From where?

Elsewhere.

I walk in darkness as yak butter
lamps, shine in the blue-eyes of gold-
cheeked Buddhas at whose knees a row
of bowls present what anyone can give,
the sheen of water in a clean bowl.
We offer up what we've been given—
a bowl of water, a sermon's silence—
responses of transparency—
and God thrives upon our thirst.

Death Dreams

I

The plumes of milkweed silk gloss the air's scent
of meadows mown in sun which slicks with shine
the swatches of house doors, strokes columbine
in window boxes and is opulent
on my face. The neat, red brick street is bent
behind me up the swell of green incline
in a world lustrous with joy's golden wine,
when the bright scrim of exaltation's rent
by the bowel knifing knowledge — I will die.
That my son will live after me doesn't buy
me solace and, despite shame's slimy maw,
my envy's acid sears to marrow's raw
truth. I stand, the street brazen with the sun,
in my death's shadow cold with oblivion.

II

It has been a long climb to this place where
the high plain opens round us in the night.
I cannot see his face — the gesturing hand
of fire between us opens from red fist
to flashing fingers — only a white-wrapped
cross-legged form. I question him. The dark
that is his face responds, "There are no answers.
I know just my pro rata of the trail."
I speak to his voice on the farside of fire,
"We grace the windings of our gowns, our hearts
beyond all breaking. Lighter of foot than

the living, none love or waltz as well as
the Dead." In my shroud's gathers rising, I say,
"There is no reason not to dance," and dance.

III

Perhaps it is Bergdorf's that I'm in or some
such store where air is thick with perfume and
obescence of clerks—an aquarium
through which exotic fish glide over sand
that's delicately dyed to match their hues.
I rub against the plushy atmosphere
luxuriating in the retinues
of comforts that suggest I'm safe, that fear
is for the poor. Lined up, the women in
the beauty salon reflect in every mirror
the daubed disguises of youth on pale skin
thin as their bones. Each is myself in terror.
Rejecting this lie's sweet breath with regret,
I fly air pockets of faith to Tibet.

The Dog's Tooth of Faith

A traveling merchant's mother asked
him to bring her a Buddha relic.
On each trip he forgot, exchanging
news over chang with friends or flirting
with nomad girls in black tents, their
braids bright with turquoise beads, or singing
love songs to mountain echoes as
he walked beside his loaded yaks.

The keeper of the family altar,
she changed the water bowls, filled butter
lamps where, with neighbors in a clutch
of houses, wind threw tantrums of dust.
She never scolded when he came
home, his bags filled with nothing but
silk, raisins, money, tea. He meant
to be a good son and felt sad.

Returning once from Lhasa he
remembered halfway home. While cursing
his thoughtlessness, he saw a dog's
jaw on the tundra, plucked a tooth
and wrapped it carefully in silk.
Smiles broke her cheeks to the deep furrows
age had plowed into her face as
she set the tooth among the lamps.

Home from the next trip he, his eyes
adjusting to the darkness, stood
inside their door and watched resolve
out of that dark his mother, friends

in meditation there before
the tooth which through its silken wrapper
glowed incandescent rainbows. His
legs also folded to the lotus.

> Half peeled potato in hand, Tashi
> says "Faith," and holds my Western eye
> with hers "makes even a dog's tooth
> shine rainbows." Childhood's saints parade
> their paste — the wine of our blood folded
> into the bread of our dust. I
> grasp a potato's gritty skin,
> a knife, and peel along with Tashi.